07

SM

NO WOMAN'S LAND

No Woman's Land

Women from Pakistan, India & Bangladesh Write on the Partition of India

Edited by
Ritu Menon

women
UNLIMITED
an associate of
Kali for women

No Woman's Land: Women from Pakistan, India & Bangladesh
write on the Partition of India
was first published in India in 2004 by

Women Unlimited
(an associate of Kali for Women)
K-36, Hauz Khas Enclave, Ground Floor,
New Delhi- 110 016

ISBN: 81-88965-04-9

Cover Design: Visual Vibe

Typeset at Print Services, B-17 Lajpat Nagar Part 2,
New Delhi 110 024, and printed at
Raj Press, R-3 Inderpuri, New Delhi 110 012

Contents

No Woman's Land

RITU MENON

The 449 km. Punjab border is lined with 600,000 landmines, laid in place over 10–15 years by the Indian government in order to contain the Punjab insurgency of the 1980s. At Hussainiwala, fields and trees stretch away into the horizon, shrouded in thick mist. In the near distance on the Indian side there is electrified fencing, great hoop of concertina barbed wire across the land. Between the international border (IB) separating India and Pakistan and the fence are strips of land cultivated by local farmers. Technically within the Indian border but outside the fencing, farmers are guarded by Border Security Force (BSF) personnel while they till their fields. Cattle, ignorant of the danger of landmines, sometimes stray across and are grievously injured. Women, who usually look after the cattle, are no longer allowed to enter those lands between the fencing and the IB, for "security reasons". For social and other reasons they can no longer relieve themselves in the fields because they are patrolled by the BSF, nor can they carry food to their menfolk when they farm their land. And whenever the army and the border villages are on high alert, villagers are told to pack up and leave with hardly any notice.

In many very particular ways, women experience the fallout of conflict swiftly and undeniably, as we know from all available accounts of current conflicts across the world. In our

part of the world, especially in the recent past and especially
in the light of high levels of ethnic violence in the entire South
Asian region, the impact is not only undeniable, it is lingering.
The fencing of the Punjab border in the west has been followed by that along the Line of Control (LoC), sometimes called
the "line of hatred" by local villagers; those who have been
trying to study border populations know how difficult it is to
sustain their enquiry because people, particularly women, are
constantly on the move. In other words, dislocated.

The Partition of India in 1947 recorded one of the most massive peace-time upheavals ever, and it is generally agreed that
its reverberations persisted and are still being felt, with vary-
ing degrees of intensity, in the three countries most affected
by it. There have been at least four major outbreaks of war
along the eastern and western borders of India, Pakistan and
Bangladesh; literally scores of skirmishes on a more or less
regular basis, some of which have flared up but stopped just
short of war; and what is called "low-intensity" warfare is an
almost constant feature in all our border areas.

Post-independence, the political history of the subcontinent
has been fairly richly and systematically documented and ana-
lysed, usually from a nationalist perspective. Subaltern and
marginal histories are now being studied more closely, but although they have contributed to decentering the historical narrative to some extent, the historical perspective remains pre-
dominantly centrist. If we were to look for a de-nationalised,
people's perspective on that epochal event, we would find it
elusive and patchy, mostly fictional, mostly male. Rarely, if ever,
has there been an attempt to present cross-border accounts
that are experiential, or that address shared concerns or histories as a consequence of 1947 and 1971; and, to the best of our
knowledge, such an offering has not yet been made from a
gendered perspective. In that sense this anthology is a first
and modest beginning, made with the hope that non-fiction
writing by Indian, Pakistani and Bangladeshi women on Partition, both contemporary and current, will open up new ways

of looking not only at what happened then, but at how lives have been lived subsequently within three new nations. Along porous borders with overlapping, sometimes conflicting and sometimes complementary, claims on identity; in situations of one's choosing, or not; with or without agency; with or without fortitude.

The weak, they say, have the purest sense of history, because they know anything can happen. The weak and the powerless, one might add. Historically speaking, women, even if not 'weak', have almost always been powerless in the larger meaning of the word, and the question that interests us here is: how does this situation influence their sense of history? It is not a question that is usually asked of women—they are presumed to be outside history because they are outside the public and the political, where history is made. Consequently, they have no part in it. At best, if unusually privileged, they may be witness to it, very rarely they may play a minor role in contributing to it; but generally they are the flotsam and jetsam of historical events—present perhaps, but of no great significance. Afterwards, they are called upon to pick up the pieces, clean up the mess, rebuild and resettle, somehow manage, somehow forgive and forget. Above all, forget. Their 'natural' inclination is to preserve, to do good works, engage in charitable and welfare activities, continue to do what they do best: nurturing and mothering. Theirs is the precinct of the personal, and once the calamity is behind them, the chaos ordered again, they withdraw from their brief foray into the public.

So what could they have to say about 1947 that hasn't already been said or fictionalised? And even if they did, how could they imbue the political with a different meaning? What exactly would their accounts tell us?

By demolishing the opposition between the personal and the political, by demonstrating that in women's experience, the personal is the political, feminism and feminist historiography have validated the importance of the experiential dimension in any analytical endeavour. Neither exclusive of all other factors, nor excluded because subjective or individual, the personal may query the political, may subvert it, may rephrase it, may even rewrite or reconfigure it.

Dadi, in Sara Suleri's essay in this book, embodies such a challenge. She simply ignored independence and Partition. "She had long since dispensed with any loyalties larger than the pitiless give-and-take of people who are forced to live together in the same place," we are told, "and she resented independence for the distances it made." With one imperious decision she dismissed the vanity of nation-making, recognising at once what it had undone in the bargain. In her eloquent, deeply moving and deeply political disquisition on "Papa and Pakistan", Dadi's granddaughter further exposes the myth of the nation—but exposes also its intrinsically male, spontaneously gendered accoutrements. The media, the military, the rhetoric, the deluding mirage of victory. Her granddaughter concludes, "That most modern thing, a Muslim nation or a Hindu nation", has no place for women, no place for her.

This no-woman's land may or may not have borders, but it does have boundaries and they are uncannily similar across national borders. In her strong desire to resist the stereotype, the crude defining of identity and allegiance, Shehla Shibli simultaneously repudiates and embraces both Hindu and Muslim. Adopts a nation, but does not barter her self, refuses to renounce one for the other. Across the expanse of India, across the eastern border, Sumati and Basanti choose—and then keep choosing as borders are drawn, disappear or are redrawn again and again. The long durée of division plays out in three generations of women, all of whom choose differently, inter-leaving gender and nation, country and community, and the compulsions of history.

Between times, however, their narratives describe the dailiness of their lives, that forgotten dimension of history in which differences are forgiven and hostilities buried. That "pitiless give-and-take" of people forced to live together blurs the boundaries between them so that choices, when they have to be made, are forced upon them by a violent disruption of the everyday, settled co-existence. A riot, a war, ethnic cleansing. Master narratives dwell on the momentous and extraordinary, reiterating them until they are normalised and internalised, thus usurping the importance of the ordinary. But marginal voices restore us to the places—and spaces—where the desultory conversations of the day are resumed and, slowly, the respite of routine restored. It is in these interstices of history that real life is resumed.

Yet it was only because Bengal was spared the long and terrifying violence of Punjab that choosing was at all possible, and changing one's mind allowed. Sumati and Basanti's intergenerational narrative unfolds a family's history, as well as national histories, on either side of the border, tracking the changing self-perception of the Bangladeshi state from secular and Bangla, to Islamic and Arabised. In an ironic reversal, what is blurred now is that sharp sense of difference between Pakistan and Bangladesh that spurred the 1971 War of Liberation: the dilution of Bengali nationalism in favour of pan-Islamism has kept the border between West and East Bengal porous as succeeding generations of those who initially stayed back, now cross over.

The relative 'peace'—by which one merely means the absence of war—of India's eastern border is in direct contrast to the turmoil in Kashmir in the west. Despite a huge military deployment along the Line of Control, border crossings by militants, extremists, civilians and others occur regularly. When hostilities between India and Pakistan abate, civilian traffic increases, with people crossing over for the day to meet relatives in Azad Kashmir (or PoK—Pakistan occupied Kashmir as the Indian government puts it), to watch cricket matches in Lahore, sometimes just to go shopping. But if, as in the recent past, all comings and goings between India and Pakistan by rail, road and air were suspended, then the only goods allowed to cross the border is dry fruit from Afghanistan.

The border town of Uri in Kashmir is a non-Kashmiri speaking tract made up mostly of Gujjars and Paharis. Luv Puri, a reporter recently in Uri, writes that a villager, Haji Assadullah, now 77 years old, has been separated from his family members, including three brothers and three sisters, since November 1947. His relatives live just 20 kms. away in Azad Kashmir. In Asida village on the Line of Control, every resident has a family member living on the other side. Bibi Jaan (72), a Gujjar woman, was married in this village before 1947 and her maternal village is two kms. across the LoC. For the last 50 years, she has not seen her two brothers and their families. With tears in her eyes she says: "We are separated by two kms. but to reach my maternal village, I have to travel hundreds of miles through the Wagah border. My financial condition did not allow me to take this route. I could not see my ailing parents before they died." She says the time has come to demolish this "line of hatred" and pass on a legacy of love to the next generation.

Ranjit Kaur's (or Jeet Masi's) story about her six-month sojourn in Muzaffarabad, in the mid-1980s, is significant in this context. Here is an ordinary Hindu couple who decide that they want to spend some time with their erstwhile neighbours and acquaintances in the city they were forced to flee in 1947. To have been able to do so more than forty years later means several things. It means that they had kept in touch; that frequent exchange visits had been taking place; that a goodly number of Hindus had converted and stayed back in Azad Kashmir; that the ties that bind communities, even mixed communities, can survive the worst violence. But they can also be severed, as the last decade of dissent in Kashmir illustrates. Now, bridging the communal divide in the Valley is one of the most urgent of peace-building activities; here, too, women have played a very important, though difficult, role.

So little is known about the Hindus and Sikhs who now call themselves Sheikhs and live in Azad Kashmir. Indeed, writing and reporting on both sides of the Kashmir border has generally been so statist and establishmentarian, so focussed on mili-

tancy or national security or migration or insurgency or freedom fighting, as the case may be, that people and their lives,
and the necessary accommodations they make, do not form
part of the historical record. Jeet Masi's starkly unadorned account of the experiences of women who were abducted is
almost shocking in its matter-of-factness, deceptive in its brev-
ity; because in her telling is encapsulated the entire gamut of
experience. Women who could never be traced, those who
resisted then finally succumbed, others whose strategies for
survival included honourable compromise—or doing violence
to their own children. Women like them challenge the very
notion of fixed identities, of birth-bound allegiances to religion and community, because their only unchanging identity
is that of womanhood. Women, as we know, have no country
and so they can make no claims on it, not even the normal,
fundamental claims of citizenship. As Kamlaben Patel's and
many other social workers' accounts make clear, women were
bartered like oranges and apples; apportioned between countries according to official classification—Hindu, Muslim, Sikh;
minor; legitimate or illegitimate; abducted or not; forcibly converted vs. voluntarily married—with no choice or rights in the
matter. Not only do women have no country, they cannot even
call their bodies their own.

A refugee's right of return, the cardinal principle of seeking
refuge and granting asylum, was never available to Partition
refugees, even though the thousands who fled at a moment's
notice, with no more than the clothes on their backs, were
sure they would return when the fury of violence abated. They
travelled by road in bullock-carts, in huge foot caravans, by
truck and train, they travelled without a destination, not knowing when, or if, they would ever arrive. On the way, they could
be relieved of whatever they might have carried—cash, jewellery, gold, food; or their wives, sisters, daughters. But still they
believed they would return. Years later, in the course of our
research, when we met widows and destituted women at the
Karnal Mahila Ashram in Haryana (India) , they still spoke of

Mianwali or Montgomery or Abbottabad or Sargodha or Multan or Sialkot as home. "Now there is no country," said Somavanti to us. "This is not ours, that is no longer ours."

Before the Ashram was set up in 1948 to look after and rehabilitate "unattached" women and children, the almost 750,000 refugees who flowed into East Punjab were housed in a refugee camp at Kurukshetra. This was the largest of about 45 camps in Punjab, a huge tented city, initially run by the army under the control of the central government. Spread over an area of about nine square miles it was divided into four townships, each with its own staff of rationing officers, store-keepers, inspectors, assistants, clerks, typists and record keepers. Jogendra Singh was a camp commandant at Kurukshetra during the first few years of its functioning, an unusual job for a young girl at the time. But calamities can also make for opportunities for women, when the breakdown of normalcy and familial protection require them to step outside the boundaries of home and hearth. There were many like Jogendra Singh, Miss Makhan Singh, Bhag Mehta, Gulab Pandit, Damayanti Sahgal, Purnima Banerji, Dr. Sushila Nayyar, Sucheta Kripalani, Bibi Amtus Salaam, Begum Anees Kidwai, Mrs. Handoo, Mrs. Shobha Nehru, Vimla Dang…

The real work of rehabilitating women fell to women; not just those whose names can be found in government records and ministry reports; not the score or more with whom we spoke but countless others, volunteers who worked in camps, in homes, in seva sadans and women's service centres as doctors, teachers, trainers, wardens, camp commandants, counsellors and companions, in the painful and protracted business of relocating and rebuilding. There were the women of the YWCA, the All India Women's Conference (AIWC), the Women's Indian Association; women who belonged to the Indian National Army, the Rashtra Sevika Samiti, the CPI and other political parties; to any number of voluntary organizations; and individual women, many themselves widowed by Partition or unmarried as a consequence of it. Some, like Anees

Kidwai persevered in the face of personal tragedy—her husband, the prominent nationalist, Shafi Ahmed Kidwai, was shot dead in Mussoorie by unknown assailants. Stunned and grief-stricken, Begum Kidwai was advised by Mahatma Gandhi to sublimate her sorrow in the service of those much worse off than her, which she did for many, many years.

The rehabilitation of refugees from the East followed a rather different course to that in the West, as has been well documented by recent studies. There is no doubt that the scale of violence in Punjab and the massive exodus of people from the West was not matched by similar upheaval and population flows in the East. It is also true that the response of the state and central governments in relief work and in the organisation of rehabilitation and the settlement of claims led to complaints of neglect and discrimination by refugees in Bengal. By the end of 1956, roughly three and a half million refugees had come into West Bengal, Assam and Tripura. Renuka Roy, Congress Member of Parliament from West Bengal, has said that "the unwillingness to accept facts and the reluctance of the Central government to rehabilitate the refugees in the east is one of the major reasons why even today the refugee problem in eastern India has not been solved". The Liaquat-Nehru Pact of 1950, according to her, was based on the assumption that the influx from East Pakistan was a temporary affair, and that both countries would encourage the return of their citizens, see that their homes and belongings were returned to them, and ensure that they could resume living without fear.

The West Bengal government, for its part, disagreed with this assumption and many in the opposition, including the Bharatiya Jan Sangh and the Communist Party of India, argued against it. Despite this, the Pact was approved but the stalemate on the ground persisted. Manikuntala Sen's is one of the few accounts we have by a woman of the time actively engaged in rehabilitation in the East, but even more importantly, possibly the only really detailed one on the impact of Direct Action Day in Calcutta in August 1946.

In spite of her horror and revulsion at the premeditated violence of that day, she says she could never be reconciled to the two-nation theory. "My birth-place (Barisal) would become another country, and my heart would break. I knew my mother, brothers, sisters and the extended family would never leave their homes and come to Calcutta as refugees... I was even more upset when I learnt that the Party (CPI) had agreed to the Partition." But she put aside her unhappiness and plunged into relief work up until her election as a member of the legislative assembly from Kalighat in 1952. She confirms observations made by other scholars of the emergence of refugee women as a political force in West Bengal, as well as the opportunity presented to them by adversity, for stepping out. Phulrenu Guha and Hasna Saha, both from erstwhile East Bengal, corroborate Manikuntala Sen's observations; and Phulrenu di makes the interesting point that the Andaman Islands could have emerged as another "East Bengal" if the West Bengal government had seriously considered it an alternative site for refuge resettlement. What strikes the reader today is the fact that, no matter how dissimilar the experiences of East and West might have been, the women who were involved with rebuilding lives used grit and imagination to overcome the odds— both government-induced and otherwise. They negotiated, subverted, manipulated or bullied, as required, to do the right thing by the women in their charge.

The great preoccupations of the human condition—freedom, nation, religion, home, friend and foe, Self and Other— are shot through with those other great themes—loss, exile, death and destruction, displacement and violence, and they compel us to look anew at those age-old borders and boundaries of nation and religion, community and identity; and at those ancient myths about shame and honour, blood and belonging. For these women who have "written" Partition, all these are open to question.

And, indeed, the difficulty of closure plagues people and nations, both. The unsettled histories of division are embodied in the figure of the refugee, the nowhere people who hover at the edges of nations, reflecting, in Tayyab Mahmud's words, "the desires and anxieties of the state". The refugee/immigrant, in his analysis, remains an outsider, an alien body, to be normalized, homogenized and assimilated. As a non-citizen, she is to be marginalized in the distribution of legal rights and political protections. As a cultural signifier, she is to be erased. As a violator of borders, she provides the rationale to ever strengthen territorial divides.

But in the Indian subcontinent, the "alien body" is often the "outsider" within, resisting assimilation and homogenization. Post-Partition, Ismat Chughtai astutely observed that, "Those whose bodies were whole had hearts that were splintered... in the end many souls remained behind in Hindustan while their bodies started off for Pakistan."

These split personalities of nations and peoples disallow reconciliation, make for a pathology of semi-permanent disease. In the end, the image of those farmers on the Punjab border ploughing their fields between barbed-wire fencing returns to haunt: refugees on their own land.

Excellent Things in Women

SARA SULERI

Dadi, my father's mother, was born in Meerut towards the end of the last century. She was married at sixteen and widowed in her thirties, and by her latter decades could never exactly recall how many children she had borne. When India was partitioned, in August of 1947, she moved her thin pure Urdu into the Punjab of Pakistan and waited for the return of her eldest son, my father. He had gone careening off to a place called Inglestan, or England, fired by one of the several enthusiasms made available by the proliferating talk of independence. Dadi was peeved. She had long since dispensed with any loyalties larger than the pitiless give-and-take of people who are forced to live together in the same place, and she resented independence for the distances it made. She was not among those who, on the fourteenth of August, unfurled flags and festivities against the backdrop of people running and cities burning. About that era she would only say, looking up sour and cryptic over the edge of her Quran, "And I was also burned." She was, but that came years later.

...

Between that phrase and the great Dadi conflagration comes the era of the trying times. They began in the winter war of 1971, when East Pakistan became Bangladesh and Indira Gandhi hailed the demise of the two-nation theory. Ifat's husband

was off fighting, and we spent the war together with her father-in-law, the brigadier, in the pink house on the hill. It was
an ideal location for antiaircraft guns, so there was a bevy of
soldiers and weaponry installed upon our roof. During each
air raid the brigadier would stride purposefully into the garden and bark commands at them, as though the crux of the
war rested upon his stiff upper lip. Then Dacca fell, and General Yahya came on television to resign the presidency and
concede defeat. "Drunk, by God!" barked the brigadier as we
sat watching. "Drunk!"

The following morning General Yahya's mistress came to
mourn with us over breakfast, lumbering in draped with
swathes of overscented silk. The brigadier lit an English cigarette—he was frequently known to avow that Pakistani cigarettes gave him a cuff—and bit on his moustache. "Yes," he
barked, "these are such trying times." "Oh yes, Gul," Yahya's
mistress wailed, "these are such trying times." She gulped on
her own eloquence, her breakfast bosom quacked, and then
resumed authority over the dangling sentence: "It is so trying,"
she continued, "I find it so trying, it is trying to us all, to live in
these trying, trying times." Ifat's eyes met mine in complete
accord: mistress transmogrified to muse; Bhutto returned from
the UN to put Yahya under house arrest and become the first
elected president of Pakistan; Ifat's husband went to India as a
prisoner of war for two years; my father lost his newspaper.
We had entered the era of the trying times.

Dadi didn't notice the war, just as she didn't really notice
the proliferation of her great-grandchildren, for Ifat and Nuzzi
conceived at the drop of a hat and kept popping babies out for
our delight. Tillat and I felt favoured at this vicarious taste of
motherhood: we learned to become that enviable personage,
a *khala*, mother's sister, and when our married sisters came to
visit with their entourage, we reveled in the exercise of *khala*-
love. I once asked Dadi how many sisters she had had. She
looked up through the oceanic grey of her cataracted eyes and
answered, "I forget".

...

After her immolation, Dadi's diet underwent some curious changes. At first her consciousness teetered too much for her to pray, but then as she grew stronger it took us a while to notice what was missing: she had forgotten prayer. It left her life as firmly as tobacco can leave the lives of only the most passionate smokers, and I don't know if she ever prayed again. At about this time, however, with the heavy-handed inevitability that characterized his relation to his mother, my father took to prayer. I came home one afternoon and looked for him in all the usual places, but he wasn't to be found. Finally I came across Tillat and asked her where Papa was. "Praying," she said. "*Praying?*" I said. "Praying," she said, and I felt most embarrassed. For us it was rather as though we had come upon the children playing some forbidden titillating game and decided it was wisest to ignore it calmly. In an unspoken way, though, I think we dimly knew we were about to witness Islam's departure from the land of Pakistan. The men would take it to the streets and make it vociferate, but the great romance between religion and the populace, the embrace that engendered Pakistan, was done. So Papa prayed, with the desperate ardor of a lover trying to converse life back into a finished love.

That was a change, when Dadi patched herself together again and forgot to put prayer back into its proper pocket, for God could now leave the home and soon would join the government. Papa prayed and fasted and went on pilgrimage and read the Quran aloud with most peculiar locutions. Occasionally we also caught him in nocturnal altercations that made him sound suspiciously like Dadi: we looked askance, but didn't say a thing. My mother was altogether admirable: she behaved as though she'd always known that she'd wed a swaying, chanting thing and that to register surprise now would be an impoliteness to existence. Her expression reminded me somewhat of the time when Ifat was eight and Mamma was urging her recalcitrance into some goodly task. Ifat postponed, and Mamma, always nifty with appropriate fables, quoted meaningfully: "'I'll do it myself,' said the little red hen." Ifat looked up with bright affection. "Good little red hen," she murmured. Then a glance crossed my mother's face, a look between a slight smile and a quick rejection of the eloquent response, like a woman looking down and then away.

She looked like that at my father's sudden hungering for God, which was added to the growing number of subjects about which we, my mother and her daughters, silently decided we had no conversation. We knew there was something other than trying times ahead and would far rather hold our breath than speculate about what other surprises the era held up its capacious sleeve. Tillat and I decided to quash our dread of waiting around for change by changing for ourselves, before destiny took the time to come our way. I would move to America, and Tillat to Kuwait and marriage. To both declarations of intention my mother said "I see," and helped us in our preparations: she knew by then her elder son would not return, and was prepared to extend the courtesy of change to her daughters, too. We left, and Islam predictably took to the streets, shaking Bhutto's empire. Mamma and Dadi remained the only women in the house, the one untalking, the other unpraying.

Dadi behaved abysmally at my mother's funeral, they told me, and made them all annoyed. She set up loud and unnecessary lamentations in the dining room, somewhat like an heir apparent, as though this death had reinstated her as mother of the house. While Ifat and Nuzzi and Tillat wandered frozen-eyed, dealing with the roses and the ice, Dadi demanded an irritating amount of attention, stretching out supine and crying out, "Your mother has betrayed your father; she has left him; she has gone." Food from respectful mourners poured in, caldron after caldron, and Dadi relocated a voracious appetite.

Years later, I was somewhat sorry that I had heard this tale, because it made me take affront. When I returned to Pakistan, I was too peeved with Dadi to find out how she was. Instead I listened to Ifat tell me about standing there in the hospital, watching the doctors suddenly pump upon my mother's heart—"I'd seen it on television," she gravely said, "I knew it was the end." Mamma's students from the university had tracked down the rickshaw driver who had knocked her down: they'd pummeled him nearly to death and then camped out in our garden, sobbing wildly, all in hordes.

By this time Bhutto was in prison and awaiting trial, and General Zulu was presiding over the Islamization of Pakistan. But we had no time to notice. My mother was buried at the nerve center of Lahore, an unruly and dusty place, and my father immediately made arrangements to buy the plot of land next to her grave: "We're ready when you are," Shahid sang. Her tombstone bore some pretty Urdu poetry and a completely fictitious place of birth, because some details my father tended to forget. "Honestly," it would have moved his wife to say.

So I was angry with Dadi at that time and didn't stop to see her. I saw my mother's grave and then came back to America, hardly noticing when, six months later, my father called from London and mentioned Dadi was now dead. It happened in the same week that Bhutto finally was hanged, and our imaginations were consumed by that public and historical dying. Pakistan made rapid provisions not to talk about the thing that had been done, and somehow, accidently, Dadi must have been mislaid into that larger decision, because she too ceased being a mentioned thing. My father tried to get back in time for the funeral, but he was so busy talking Bhutto-talk in England that he missed his flight and thus did not return. Luckily, Irfani was at home, and he saw Dadi to her grave.

Bhutto's hanging had the effect of making Pakistan feel unreliable, particularly to itself. Its landscape learned a new secretiveness, unusual for a formerly loquacious people. This may account for the fact that I have never seen my grandmother's grave and neither have my sisters. I think we would have tried, had we been together, despite the free-floating anarchy in the air that—like the heroin trade—made the world suspicious and afraid. There was no longer any need to wait for change, because change was all there was, and we had quite forgotten the flavor of an era that stayed in place long enough to gain a name. One morning I awoke to find that, during the course of the night, my mind had completely ejected the names of all the streets in Pakistan, as though to assure that I could not return, or that if I did, it would be returning to a loss. Overnight the country had grown absentminded, and patches of amnesia hung over the hollows of the land like fog.

... For to be lost is just a minute's respite, after all, like a train that cannot help but stop between the stations of its proper destination in order to stage a pretend version of the end. Dying, we saw, was simply change taken to points of mocking extremity, and wasn't a thing to lose us but to find us out, to catch us where we least wanted to be caught. In Pakistan, Bhutto rapidly became obsolete after a succession of bumper harvests, and none of us can fight the ways that the names Mamma and Ifat have become archaisms, quaintnesses on our lips.

Sara Suleri was born to a Welsh mother and a Pakistani father who was a prominent political journalist of his times. She teaches English at Yale University and is the author of *Meatless Days*, *Boys Will Be Boys* and *The Rhetoric of English India*.

Excerpted from Sara Suleri, Meatless Days *(Chicago: University of Chicago Press), 1989.*

Papa and Pakistan

SARA SULERI

There were always a few words that his flamboyant English insisted he mispronounce: words, I often imagined, over which his heart took hidden pleasure when he had got them by the gullet and held them there until they empurpled to the color of his own indignant nature. "Another" was one of them—I cannot count how many times each day we would hear him say, "Anther?" "Anther?" It did not matter whether it was another meal or another government or another baby at issue: all we heard was a voice bristling over with amazement at the thought that anther could exist. It seemed his patience could not sustain itself over the trisyllablic, tripping up his voice on most trisyllables that did not sound like "Pakistan"—for there was a word over which he could slow down, to exude owner-ship as he uttered it! But something like "beginning"—that is, something more mundane—had to become "bigning," a hasty abbreviation that was secretly aware of the comic quality of slapdash, the shorthand through which slapdash begins. He was a journalist, after all. We of course could only listen, with loyal cells producing their precious moisture almost at the pace at which that large voice was speaking, suspecting itself, and then dismissing suspicion to talk on and on. How was it pos-sible for us, chosen audience of those locutions, not to listen with our spirits on our lips, thrilling with compassion? It was

not possible, and told us of the way our days designed themselves to be. For in the bigning, there was Pip.

They must have hit upon their names in about the same
era, that decade of the 1930s, when Ziauddin—a Rajput
Salahria, employee of the imperial government in India—decided to become Z.A. Suleri the writer, and some Indian Muslims in England decided it was high time to talk about Islamic
independence and invented that new coinage, Pakistan. The
word emerged from Cambridge, actually, where a group of
three students published a small pamphlet entitled "Now or
Never," followed by the winning subtitle "Are We to Live or
Perish Forever?" It always struck me as a particularly Pakistani
question, combining as it did the obvious with umbrage and
ignoring the fact that "now" is a tricky word, embedded in the
oblique. At the time of its publication Papa must have moved
to Delhi to live with his aunt after his father died: there he
became a civil servant, and how his spirit chafed at the recollection of those days! He would get up in the morning in despair, thinking of all the other mornings he would also have to
rise, take the same road to the same office, and look forward
to nothing more than coming home again. "Was that to be the
compass of my life?" he thundered, glaring at me as though I
were at least the aunty who had conjured him to remain in
such respectable employ. I did not deserve his glare, for my
spirit quite cheered at the thought of him giving up his job and
writing poems and, with his cousin Shamim, peddling film
scripts all the way from Delhi to Bombay. But Pip was always
a wonderful consumer of context: he would eat it up alive, just
like a cannibal, so no audience that came his way departed
without feeling slightly stripped. It was hardly simple, playing
the part of never to his now, but then which good humor would
not soften at the manifest satisfaction with which he ate?

He ate up his past, too, in the manner of a nervous eater, so
that my attempts to establish some sense of the narrative of his
days always filled me with a sense of uneasy location. There
were some stories he told wonderfully, and we were trotted

over them with all the expansiveness of people who conglom-
erate for the exclusive joy of traversing, once again, familiar
terrain. But establishing the sequence of those stories was a
less easy thing to do, and for some years I would chide myself
for owning an absentminded brain, a faculty so distracted that
it could not even retain the structure of my father's life as part
of its water table's constant. But then I noticed all the detail he
had to forget in order to pay vociferous attention to his now,
and saw that it was not my proper task to be divining out the
silence of his streams. Still, he could surprise me. "Mamma," I
asked once, after an evening filled with his wonderful stories,
"why does Papa call his grandmother his 'elder mother'?" A
quick change of manner crossed her face. "Oh, my dear," she
said slowly, "he isn't talking about his grandmother: he's talking about his father's other wife." I realized then that there
would always be mirages in his eyes for me, who had no way
of knowing all the ground he must have covered to domesticate his life.

My Dadi should have given me a clue, of course. But she,
that most imperious soul, was not a woman much given to
intimate chitchat, far preferring to praise God or curse men
instead. She came from Meerut—heart of Urdu-speaking land—
and was somehow married to my grandfather, a Punjabi Rajput
from Sialkot who evidently had several wives. His name was
Allah Baksh, and I have never quite deciphered what he actually did to keep himself employed. And so we would question
Siraj Din, a relative from my grandfather's village, when he
came up to visit us in Lahore; but Siraj Din was no help at all.
"Oh, he was very pious," he assured us solemnly, "a very pious man." I further gleaned that he was fond of traveling, and,
in the last quarter of the last century went all the way to Mecca
to do as a Muslim should his Hajj, returning to have the first
brick mosque built in his Sialkot village—Deovli, it is called.
Then he spent much time in the princedoms of Deccan, that
region of India slightly south of the north, and my father told
me stories of all that he would and would not do when he

visited him as a child in the princely houses. Beyond that, however, I cannot imagine what my grandfather did, apart from
having several wives. "He loved to ride camels!" Papa once
said, appreciatively, at which point I just gave up. "Wait! My
grandfather," I said steadily, "was fifty years old when he married that slip of a thing, my Dadi at sixteen, his second wife.
Beyond that, he liked to ride camels—am I right?" Papa looked
up, surprised at such unnecessary interruption: "Why, yes!" he
simply said.

But when was Pip in one place long enough for us to walk
over him scientifically, his past our archaeological site? If anything, he was in too many places at once, recounting different
histories for each, which overwhelmed us with the clamor they
made for his complete attention. And I have no reason to believe that he was ever different, even in the era of his youth
when he decided that his life must write. So he moved from
Delhi to Lahore and went back to the university, earning one
degree in Persian and anther in journalism, torn as he was between the literary and the political, uncertain on which to land.
In later years he would tell me with a sigh, "I did myself dis-
service when I gave up my tongue." But a young man of his
times hardly had a choice when he found himself seduced by
history but to give up Urdu or Hindi in the service of English,
which was history's language then. Generations of Urdu conversation in his genes must have shuddered with desertion as
Papa's imperatives sent him off, away from poetry, into an English daily. He adopted it with a Dickensian zeal, picking up
phrases and tonalities that he would never lose: he always
talked about newspapers as dailies, as morningers or
eveningers, for "newspaper" was a reader's word. He was
happy, then, feeling at the hub of himself and of history, and
shortly thereafter was to feel happier still. For then he met
Jinnah.

Consider Papa, growing up in a part of northern India known
as Quadian, born in 1913 when his father was approaching
sixty, first seduced by poetry, and then by history. What else

could he do when he met Jinnah but exclaim, "Amazing grace!" Jinnah was an actor, certainly the most aware of all the politicians of India at that time of how to maintain a poetical posture in its history. So Pip became a person swamped in the true devotion of his soul, working in the service of what he could only name perfection. And he named it, constantly: he saw to it that I grew up in a world that had only a single household god, called the Quaid, so that even today I feel slightly insolent to my upbringing when reality prompts me to call him by his real name, Jinnah. It is a curious epithet, the Quaid, that—after he had manhandled the country into being—Pakistan adopted to call the Leader, but in our home that title conveyed an added twist, becoming in Pip's impassioned discourse nothing other than the Father. No wonder I never learned more details of my grandfather, I mused, when Papa had thus named the Quaid and then veered off into his rapturous litany of desire. But what an odd man to make familial: gaunt with elegance and intellect, the discourse of a barrister imprinted on his brain, Jinnah the maker of Pakistan was hardly an easy idea to domesticate—and yet Pippy did it. He loved everything about that man: his design, his phrase, his clothes.

At that point, Papa was married to Baji, Nuzzi's mother. She was his cousin, and since earliest recall—when they were running round in some infant game—he knew as he watched her gambols, "That cousin is my wife." For so it had been decreed, and their marriage must have been quite a celebratory event, although Pip has never described it to me. Baji was a child, my father twenty-five, when after college in Layallpur he was married to her. The next year, Nuz was born: they were such impassioned days for Pip that he could only name his daughter Nuzhat Shelley Suleri, to mediate between his inchoate regard for her and for Percy Bysshe. It made us weep with laughter when, decades later, Nuz confessed to us how she had been named: no wonder you are such a comic spirit, we told her, for how could a life abstain from comedy after having its middle name signed over to Percy Bysshe? Baji must have been tolerant in those days to have allowed her baby to carry such a name, and Nuz strong to sustain her birthing and the events that followed shortly after. Indeed so, since the next year was the year of the Lahore Resolution.

When at the beginning of the century Jinnah turned from law to politics, the modernity of his mind naturally inclined him into becoming—as he was called—the Ambassador of Hindu-Muslim Unity. But the logic of arguing for independence unleashed odd thoughts in India, so that in 1930 the poet Iqbal's Allahabad Address to the Muslim League could contain visionary references to the idea of a separate Indian Muslim nation. Jinnah was more pragmatic, however, when he turned to that opinion. "To me, Hindus, Muslims, Parsis, Harijans are all alike," Gandhi declared, "I cannot be frivolous when I talk of Quaid-i-Azam Jinnah. He is my brother." "The only difference is this," Jinnah replied, "that brother Gandhi has three votes and I have only one vote." It was that imbalance in parity which led, in 1940, to the Lahore Resolution, when the Muslim League met in Lahore on the twenty-third of March and drafted the Pakistan Declaration. What a strange occasion it must have been: crowds of hundreds of thousands gathering in the open field next to the Badshahi Mosque, of which how many understood the two-hour speech that Jinnah rose to give, prefaced with the calm disclaimer, "The world is watching us, so let me have your permission to have my say in English"? "It has always been taken for granted that the Mussalmans are a minority, and we have got used to it for such a long time that these settled notions sometimes are very difficult to remove," Jinnah told that crowd in Lahore. "The Mussalmans are not a minority. The Mussalmans are a nation by any definition." Papa was in that crowd, of course, listening rapturously.

So, freshly fathered, Papa moved to Karachi in 1941 to join the weekly *Dawn* as a subeditor until it became a daily in 1943. Then he went to Lahore and the *Orient Press* as its Lahore editor: in that year, 1944, he wrote his first book, *The Road to Peace and Pakistan*. The next year, he wrote anther. Called

My Leader, it combined a certain Carlylian hero-worship with an intuitively shrewd sense of political pragmatics. The book gave Pip some fame, but—even more—it gave him what in the years of my formation was referred to only as "the Letter": to this day it remains the one object in Pip's home that he has ever loved. "It is very encouraging to me indeed." Jinnah wrote, "that a man like you should have such a warm and affectionate corner for me." ("If this is a corner," I interpolated to Ifat, "what on earth does the centre look like?") "I congratulate you on marshalling facts so well and giving a clear picture of the seven years of our struggle." Years later, I would think reproachfully about that phrase and the ideas it put into Papa's head, because he has been martialing facts ever since. He would forget that we weren't facts and would martial us too, up and down the nation.

The royalties from *My Leader* gave Papa an idea: he would go to England and propagate what he called the Pakistan Cause in the capitals of Europe. He went to Bombay to get Jinnah's blessing, and in 1945 bought a passage to England. He left Baji and Nuz with Baji's parents, and then he set sail. It must have been strange for him, arriving alone in London, learning the lay of another land: "I spent most of the day around Whitehall," he wrote years later, "attending briefings and press conferences in the Foreign and Commonwealth offices and in the lobbies of the House of Commons. At that time, I was the lone 'Pakistani' correspondent in Britain—'Pakistani' before Pakistan, because I didn't attend any of these gatherings without raising the issue of the Muslim struggle for Pakistan." I believe it, when I read it; it has the ring of veracity, particularly when his next sentence swerves off to add, in his charming fashion, "In my one unchanging blue suit I became a familiar figure among the journalists and politicians, and my busy-bee movements galled the bulging band of my Hindu counterparts, who had monopolized the scene for decades." But Papa could not have been at Whitehall all the time, for the next year he met my mother.

How could he do it, be so absentminded as to forget he already had a wife and daughter? There was always an alacrity to his switch of allegiance, but at least Allah Baksh was in his grave when Jinnah superseded him. They talked well together, it seems—Mamma at twenty-five must have been a talking thing—but I would hardly have thought that sufficient for him to pick up ten years of his life with Baji and just put it in his pocket. Oh, knowing his makeup I have no doubt he sang with pain, but he went through with it anyway. The divorce was conducted by mail, and in Karachi Nuz at nine was told that her grandparents were her parents, that Baji was her sister. You, Nuz, you knew that falsehood signified a grave composure: you took that gravity and worked upright to build on it the clarity of your smile, your laugh.

But 1947 saw another break: the break of Britain leaving the shores of India, that place of many countries, many people, which they had just tidied in two! In London, Papa pulled out his Muslim League flag and at some public ceremony was asked to unfurl it, giving him what he later called the most moving moment of his life. Today I often regret that he was not in Pakistan at the time of the partition, to witness those bewildered streams of people pouring over one brand-new border into another, hurting as they ran. It was extravagant, history's wrenching price: farmers, villagers, living in some other world, one day awoke to find they no longer inhabited familiar homes but that most modern thing, a Muslim or a Hindu nation. There was death and panic in the cities when they rose up to flee, the Muslims traveling in one direction, the Hindus in the other. I wish, today, that Pip had been a witness of it all: surely that would have given him pause and conferred the blessing of doubt? But he was still in postwar London, living with my mother now, although Baji may well have been a semblance of the question in his head when he sat down to write *Whither Pakistan?* Mamma says that Papa wept the following year, when Jinnah died. I am sure that he wept every day for that fund of free-floating worship in his soul until, in 1949, Mamma gave birth to Ifat.

What followed were the days of information, times so hectic that my mind tires in advance at the prospect of type-setting them. My parents returned to Karachi, with Ifat the object of their delight, but they returned to the absence of relatives in a culture studiously conscious of the posture of relation. Mamma was probably still too new, too puzzled, to notice it, but Pip must have uttered a great good-bye to the extended family of Pakistan before he cast himself with renewed ferocity into the printing of its news. It was as though his life was determined to be as novel as the nation, so he started a new newspaper, the *Evening Times*. For the next several years Pip kept himself preoccupied by inventing newspapers and procreating: Shahid was born in the year that the *Evening Times* became a morninger; the *Times of Karachi* and I followed close behind. By this time I know my mother must have had an inkling of it all, but she loved her babies and didn't seem to mind. I wish I had been there, however, or in a state of greater consciousness, on the occasion of Nuzzi's first visit to us, when, turning to my father, "Sir, you have such beautiful babies!" she exclaimed. She and Mamma regarded one another sorrowfully, Nuz tells me, and then without a word decided to convert into a shared responsibility their portions of guilt and loss. I can attest they were each others' closet friends in the years I grew up with Ifat and Shahid.

What sounds of conversation filled my infancy, patters of urgent and perpetual talk! I heard my parents talking to each other all the time, but never of themselves, only about newspapers and circulations and odd names like Khwaja Nazimuddin and Mr. Laiquat Ali. For there was still a parliament in Pakistan: an abundant, talk-filled era, long before we had developed with such gusto our taste for censorship and martial law. So prime ministers came and went, and Pip was in and out of jail: it made Ifat sob dramatically, "Oh, no, no, he's not a jailbird, not Papa!" But life had a centre, like a printing press, constantly in motion. So when Papa was jailed for sedition, during my gestation, and Mamma was in charge of the *Times of Karachi*, she made her protest known. She ordered into press an empty paper, sheafs of blank newsprint that bore nothing but the title, the *Times of Karachi* and the burden of nude paper. Karachi citizens must have been left quite perplexed, picking up their papers on the following morning and finding nothing but barren newsprint. "She made them know how angry she was when she turned censorship into sedition!" Papa would exclaim in later years, gazing at his wife in proud regard, "Her drama added six months to my sentence!" Then he was in jail for what felt like the longest time for me, after we had moved to Lahore and Pip was imprisoned for the Gurmani case. It was either for libel or sedition—one of those words that possessed our infant imaginations—so that it did not matter to me that I had no idea who Gurmani was when Ifat and Shahid and I sat down to draw hideously vicious little representations of the man and send them off to Papa to cheer him up in jail.

I missed him when he was gone. But Papa's delight in his babies often implied that they were a respite after he had dealt with the day's true significance. As a result we stood like curious animals, urging one another to step forward in examination, to stalk round and to sniff the great machine at the heart of things from which we were a respite. It had a manufacturer's name emblazoned on one side: when we learned how to read, we bent down and spelled out "h-i-s-t-o-r-y." That was the author of it all, we thought, when Pip emerged from jail and found General Ayub in charge, the parliament disbanded: it made him decide that he had had his fill of editing for a while and should look for something different. So he became a foreign correspondent once again and shipped us off to England. Before we left, Mamma had another child, a little girl called Tillat, whose vastness of eye and absence of nose entranced us all, although Mamma was getting fatigued.

Papa felt odd about living in England, as though he were a minority once more, a person absented from the functioning of what he himself had built. He wrote, however, with a ferocity of soul, sending off dispatch after dispatch, so that in place of the clanking of a printing press the music of our day changed to Papa on the telephone. "*R* Robert, *E* Edward, *D* Dover," he would shout to some long-suffering telegraph service. And he wrote another book, called *Pakistan's Lost Years*, for he was developing a glimmering fear that perhaps the country would completely forget what it means to be historical. I think Pip feared for his progeny as well. One day he glanced up from his work to stare at Ifat intently, who was at that phase in life when being stared at is dangerous. We were growing, he noticed, into a dangerous phase—what choice had he but to make Mamma pack our bags again and return to Pakistan, to forestall us lest we become totally possessed by someone else's history? Before we left, Irfan was born. My mother was very fatigued.

Pakistan had changed during General Ayub's Decade of Development, which was still in full swing when we returned. There was more of the army in the air, of course, more uniformity around to censor discourse. So many newspapers had been nationalized that to be an editor was tantamount to working for the government. Papa's spirit rose up in rebellion at this; his first brief tenure as editor of the *Pakistan Times* was filled with storm and ire. I never learned to like the building in Lahore which housed that enormous paper: it clattered so, with people constantly rushing up and down its hallways, ink-damp galleys in their hands. We were to see enough of it, nonetheless, in the next twenty years, during which Pip by turns edited the paper and then was ousted; reappointed, and ousted again. For though the governments and information secretaries did not like him much, Pip's name—like his presence—had a weight, and they had to admit he was competent. I sometimes wished that he were less competent, ready to become instead a sager, quieter soul: but how could that happen when history, dressed as the *Pakistan Times*, was waiting for him, beckoning him into the longest romance of his life?

Odd, to think that just one man could keep us all so busy. There we were, attendant on his tempestuous career, waiting like proofreaders to go through the galleys of his days, breathless with surprise. He certainly surprised us during the 1965 war, when he offered his services to the government and headed the military public relations service as a colonel in the Pakistan army. He had wonderful stories of those days, of course, of his struggles with his uniform, of how he would zoom up and down the border in a little helicopter, landing next to indifferent farming folk and shouting out, "Where's the war?" We knew he could not last in that environment long and expected him to be out again, founding another paper or returning to the *Pakistan Times*. Those were heady days in Pakistan, with Ayub's empire beginning to crumble and the horizon brightening at the prospect of an alternative, a man called Zulfikar Ali Bhutto. For a while Bhutto and Pip were the closet of friends, but something in their forms of power clashed, making them mistrust each other's version of history. "Ah, Suleri, Suleri," sighed Bhutto when they met, "now all we have left in common are our initials." Papa laughed, because then he was very fond of him, but that was soon to change.

How different Pakistan would be today if Ayub had held elections at that time, in 1968, instead of holding on until the end and then handing power over to—of all people!—Yahya. But military governments, although utterly efficient at starting to rule, do not usually know how to stop—except, of course, General Yahya's government, which held an election and, not knowing how to face its consequences, clamped a massive military emergency on a single province that led not just to its secession but to the bloody war of Bangladesh. If Ayub had held elections there might still have been a deathly power struggle between Bhutto and Mujib: Mujib, the elected leader of East Pakistan; Bhutto, of West Pakistan. There probably would have been a Bangladesh anyway, but maybe with less blood.

Back at the *Pakistan Times*, Pip watched events like a man possessed: he wrote night and day and would not believe it when, during the 1970 election, his workers went out on strike. "The nation is going through a crisis, and you think of a raise?" he thundered to the union representatives. "Is that the yardstick of your devotion?" Apparently it was not, since the strike was soon called off.

With the country absorbing every moment of his attention, Papa thought it was highly unreasonable of his children to distract him from his proper duty by behaving as though they had lives. When Nuz got married, Papa would not speak to her for years. It was all because Baji understandably did not want him to attend the wedding—a small courtesy, you would think, but sufficient to put Pip into a major miff. At the time I did not realize that I was witnessing the formation of a pattern, but—it turns out—after each of his daughter's weddings something in Pip's soul maintains a shuddering silence at the thought of them until, finally, he manages to look up, a mighty resignation in his eyes. The second crisis—an enormous one—came when Ifat decided to marry a polo-playing army man: "But what does he know," Papa asked in horror, "about the genesis of Pakistan?" He still believed he had a veto power over his children's lives, but Ifat was hardly a woman to veto, even when she was six. After Ifat went and married the man, Pip would not let her name be mentioned in his presence, so total was her banishment. They came to an uneasy reconciliation some two years later, but for a while we missed her sorely, hungry for her presence in our lives.

By the time Ifat was allowed to visit us again, my mother's sympathy had trained me to be the second person in the home to decipher my father's impossible hand. It cut out a new task for my afternoons, when I would sit with a Men and Matters article next to me, transcribing into a florid copper-plate Papa's ferocious language. His typists and typesetters could read only curly handwriting, so I forced my *g*'s to curl. "The Jamaat-i-Islami opposed the Pakistan movement tooth and nail," I copied out, "it was only after partition that the party changed its colors and Maudoodi reared his ugly head." "Are you sure that isn't libel, Pip?" I asked him doubtfully. Or Mamma and I would look at each other in dismay when Papa called us from his office to command, "Mairi, Sara, about two years ago I wrote an article called 'Whither Basic Democracy?' Find it for me, please." So we would turn to those great sheaves of paper, impossible to file, to hunt and hunt through that familiar discourse for the words of his desire. I did not like to have to handle so much newspaper and sometimes felt as though my fingerprints were wearing out with the impact of all that ink.

But something of our spirits broke, in the war of 1971. It was not so much the country's severing that hurt as the terrible afterimages we had to face: censorship lifted for a flash, flooding us with photographs and stories from the foreign press of what the army actually did in Bangladesh during the months of emergency that preceded the war. "I am not talking about the two-nation theory," I wept to my father, "I am talking about blood!" He would not reply, and so we went our separate ways, he mourning for the mutilation of a theory, and I—more literal—for a limb, or a child, or a voice. Bhutto came to power after the war in Bangladesh, making Pip say darkly, "If he had negotiated, if he had conceded, this would not have happened". Even Bhutto had lost some of the jauntiness that had so won the heart of the electorate of West Pakistan: "Yes, I drink!" he had told his entranced Muslim audience, "But I also work, don't I?" Or in the midst of a formal reception he would choose to join the performers on the stage, to dance and sing with them, "He jamalo, ho jamalo!" Our days were more bitter, though, when Bhutto inaugurated his autocratic rule: Papa left the *Pakistan Times*, becoming the government's most vocal critic.

Now we were in trying times. Ifat's husband was a prisoner of war, putting clouds about her face, clearing only in moments when we talked and watched her two children play. Papa took to praying, which he had never done before; one day I looked up to notice a graying in his eyes and realized in sharp premonition, "Why, Pip is growing blind." History was turning his eyes inward, and even though it was an operable, curable disease, for years we had to wince at the sudden hesitance in his bold stride. "Honestly, Mamma," I couldn't help but grumble, "you'd think he could have chosen a less Miltonic ailment." "Honestly, Sara!" she said in reply.

But we were coming to a parting, Pakistan and I. I felt supped full of history, hungry for flavors less stringent of my palate, less demanding of my loyalty. Ifat told me that she always knew I had to go, "But I don't want to be in the same room when you tell Pip!" she added ruefully. I did not much want to be there myself, did not want to see how scandalized his face would be at the thought that I could thus rob myself of the abundance of his company. It cost me a curious sum of courage when I sat with him through that conversation. For a while he looked at me as though I were telling him that I was not a nation any more, that I was a minority: then, slowly, his face crossed over into dignity. "If I say no, you still will go," he told me quietly. "Go, child. I have no choice."

My mother helped me pack my books; Tillat and Ifat chose my clothes; Irfani found a piece of wood and carved an ashtray for me. Even Allah Ditta the cook stopped grumbling on the morning that I left, saying to me almost fondly, "Who will give me the daily order now?" "Keep on living," Dadi said and barely kissed my head. "The thing that makes me happiest," Mamma wrote to me shortly after, "is the thought of your life." For they were glad to have me gone into some other difference, a world of fewer deadlines, less notoriety. I in the American Midwest woke up to find myself inhabiting an unreal little town that looked to me like toy-land: my hours of rest were happy truants then, filling me with glee. I woke in the morning without a paper at my door and blessed the peace that put me out of it, the endless circulation of news. My life told me that it had long been waiting for this weekend when it could stay in bed: so stay put, then, life, I said, and brought it breakfast too. Of course I also missed my duties, though I would not admit it, and gradually noticed that I did take an interest in the fate of Bhutto's empire: to read that there was rioting in Lahore suddenly made me shiver, to think I was not there. Still, I was happy for a year, even when I caught myself peering around for information in the manner of Pip's Miltonic eyes.

Poor Ifat, she had so many duties in those days, tending to Papa during his two eye operations and then to Mamma in the wicked March she died! Mamma was crossing the road from the university where she taught over to Tollington Market when a rickshaw driver came to knock her down and bruise her from her mind. In the days she teetered on her own brink, she came to consciousness once: she smiled at Ifat, saying strangely, "Send the car for the children, Zia." When I met Ifat later that summer, she solemnly told me all her tales: "When I saw the doctor pump upon her heart—it's the kind of thing you see on television—I knew it was the end." "Oh, Ifat," I mourned to her, "god help us for the way that information comes!" Papa of course was prostrate, broken. I saw fear in him then, for the first time ever, as though my mother's absence made him immediately more parochial, uncertain that the present was a place he could again inhabit. I watched his face struggle with its grief, and felt a deep compassion when I saw how unerringly his mind led him to its only trick of solace, for Papa was not trying to understand how quickly grief becomes its own memorial: he was fighting it instead, and trying to forget.

By that time, Bhutto had been deposed and Zulu Haq was in power. Papa returned to the *Pakistan Times,* and I think that last stint of editing gave him great relief, filling his days again with the great reality of newsprint. But 1979 was a strange year in many ways, for first of all our Dadi died, and then they did in Bhutto. When Zulu Haq took over and Bhutto was imprisoned, I had imagined that he would end like those others—Yahya and Ayub—living out his days under house arrest. It disquieted me, then, when he was put on trial for murder in a case that seemed inexorably bound to stop before the thought of clemency, since we already knew the verdict. Laws were changing in Pakistan, and I had a dread that the country was prepared to consume the last vestiges of its compassion. Away in America, I cringed to hear the unseemly news that Bhutto had been hanged. What had happened to the memory of those minds, I thought, that they could so abuse a body that they once had loved? I could feel that a brute energy was building up in Pakistan, as though the ghost of that populace—mercilessly cast about in 1947, then again in 1971—had summoned up its strength again, but this time for revenge. On us, at least, the vengeance came.

Ifat died precisely a day after the second anniversary of my mother's death. She was walking with her husband outside her home in Lahore when a car drove up and knocked her down and then vanished without a trace. By the time I got back to Pakistan, it was as though I did not have even the idea of a sister any more, for Ifat had become the news. Her name was everywhere, a public domain, blotting out her face and its finesse into the terrible texture of newsprint. The mourners who came visiting us seemed quickened with hungry curiosity: I stood by speechless as I watched the world sensationalize her life, her death. And then came the murder case, endless investigations that led nowhere but to greater trouble to our souls. It was Papa's enemies, they said. No, it was the family, they said. I sat with Tillat and Shahid and Pip in silence, our hearts afflicted. Our minds were not relieved to know that Ifat had written me a letter the day before she died: oh, it felt grotesquely clumsy, waiting for that letter to be forwarded from America, to see what Ifat said! Her words to me were sweet, and they spoke about her life, so that—for me—their reading was almost a reprieve, suggesting endless possibility of conversation still in store for us. "Be rational, Sara!" Shahid whispered to me. "That's not a letter to you now—it's evidence," he said. Ifat's letter, evidence? I said a quick good-bye to the sweet assurance of those days when I could claim to know the name of things. At that moment, privacy left our lexicon: it surely left my life.

Evidence or not, the letter did not help, and slowly we came to admit to ourselves that our nightmare of detection would not have an end, leaving us always ignorant of its most vital information. Pakistan was very ready to forget: the news had been sensational, but now its day was done. At home, however, we moved round in slow despair, our practice of habit broken. There was no behavior in my mind that did not require painstaking reformulation: how do I lift this glass, I'd think, and take it to my lips? Our only solace was to tend to Ifat's children, three of them now: the youngest, Ayesha, turned six. But Pip was a person deranging through those days, working in rage to reconstruct the semblance of a thought, and in a forgetful trick I could not understand that he made a separation in his head between himself and Ifat's children. "They belong to their father," he told us angrily, "you cannot interfere." I was amazed to think that he, who had seen families swallowed up before, could expect us also to construct this roughest judgement. "When you go back to America, there's hardly much that you'll do for the children," Shahid told me, "maybe Papa's right." But Shahid, my mind whispered, you just were not here. These mites were not fragments in your hands when they were hours old: you have not felt the funniness with which they grow and grow. You ask me to repudiate, now she is freshly dead, the things of Ifat's life? But he could not respond to what I did not say. And so my silence hissed to me: stay, in the face of history, harbor to those three most deserving of a cove, since they have lost delicious wind that gave them their desire—or go, but know that you leave with a body derogate, unfit in such desertion to conceive even the idea of a child! Back and forth I went, bandying between the proper duty of my grief: to whom did I owe my allegiance, those who were grieving or the object of that grief? My mind fatigued itself in the anguish of that shilly-shally. And then, I did not stay.

I returned to America conscious of my vanity, the gay pretense with which I had believed that I could take a respite from my life. It was only then that I became historical, a creature gravely ready to admit that significance did not sit upon someone else's table like a magazine to which one could or could not subscribe. I listened to the chattering of my ghosts and told them, "Soft you, I have done the state some service, and you know it." Then I waited for the chastisement I knew I deserved: "You were the state, and yet you did not know!" Oh my mind's fool, I thought, astonished: it has taken you the deaths of a dear mother and a dear sister, the loss of three dear children, before you could contemplate such a dangerous simplicity? You were born fit; you rendered yourself unfit. Now comes the time when you must make yourself historical.

An impossible act, however, to explain to Pip, who needed badly to retain his version as the only form of history. Pip was very gentle when we next met, in Williamstown, where I had packed away my life of lazy Sundays and now begun to work. He would not look on me as on a renegade, sending instead old stories circulating between us, familiars that I was glad to have for company. Of course he was going to write his memoirs, he announced, and call it *Boys Will Be Boys*: he knew how that title made me laugh. We talked of politics rather than of my return, while the names of our dead hung about us like the atmosphere in which we breathed and spoke. I trounced the Islamization of Pakistan to him; he trounced it back to me. "The genesis of Pakistan was not Islam!" he shouted, as I knew he would, "It was different—it was Muslim nationhood!" All the while I knew he still believed that it was possible for me to go back and to live with him, reluctant as he was to read the "never" in my eyes. "Do you ever have sensations of daughterly compunction?" he asked me, touchingly. "Sometimes, Papa," I breathed, "I do." Then he took pity on me, and brightened up his tone to tell me once again his favorite story of my babyhood. He had returned from Europe late in the night and on a warm Karachi morning was happy to be sitting in his room again, kissing us one by one as we got up. I was the last to awake and came bustling into his bedroom with great welcome, announcing myself as I ran in, "Another girl!" I could never quite see why that story had such meaning for him, but to Pip it defined my life. "Anther girl, anther girl!" he repeated to me in Williamstown, bright laughter on his face.

Did he have an inkling then, when Pip went back to Pakistan alone, a dreadful thought to him? He had his paper still, to preoccupy both night and day with deadline's sweet familiarity, but history was not sufficient then to keep the demons from his soul. Burying my mother had been bad enough, but burying Ifat in the gravespace where he hoped to lie was terrifying, making his bed each night a place where he must work to bury her again. I mourned to imagine the extremity of that labor, wondering when it would compel him to forgetfulness, his old luxurious habit. What I did not know was that this work was also making Papa feel the need to be historical: one day he gave a mighty sob, arose, and glanced around Lahore. Then he found himself another daughter. It was a contingency that had not occurred to me, until I got Nuzzi's letter. I was glad that I heard it from her and that her unpunctuation made me see the humor of this astounding information: "Irfani is the Sherlock Holmes in this," Nuzzi scrawled, "But it has been in the papers too so Sara you must know that Papa's adopted a daughter and we have a new sister now." "Anther girl, indeed!" I exclaimed. "I asked him why he hadn't remarried because I thought he had enough daughters already but he did not really reply." "Ah, Papa," I thought, "you have laughed tears to my eyes, for even if you had worked on it for years—albeit unknowingly—you could not have hit upon a more adequate revenge!" I shook my head throughout the day, until that evening Shahid called: "You've heard what's happened, I suppose." I told him that although I'd always known that Pip was brilliant at fresh starts, such a bigning was big enough to take my breath away. "In terms of the limit, it is quite Pippish," was all that Shahid had left to say. We shook our heads in unison over the phone at this preponderance of reality. "And then the name," he added, "the strangeness of the name." "What is the name?" I asked him, interested. Shahid gave a transatlantic shiver. "She's called Shahida!" he said.

Thus it happened that I was distracted once again—long after I thought I had outlived such moments of interruption—to ponder in slow thought the amazement of that man. With professional efficiency, as though orchestrating governmental change, Pip cleared the family stage of his mind and ushered a new one in. It made me admit that I would never be immune to the exigencies of information: in Pakistan, the propriety of every eyebrow raised itself at Pip, whose publicity insisted that this was his play, both to direct and to act in. What could we do, we asked one another, but applaud, as though we were applauding the tragic failure of farce? Historical myself, it made me recognize the soil that Pip was asserting when, on my next visit to Pakistan, I found him in the Punjabi pink, his brand-new daughter by his side. Weeping for my dead was quite another issue: his demeanor made me look at him quizzically, and he looked at me gruffly, so that for the first time in years the airspace between us was rife with comedy again. "I have my needs," he snarled when we were once alone. "You do, indeed," I answered seriously. Then his face fell away from its defense into a quick crossing of dignity: "It was just a matter of shamelessness and fatigue, simply that," he sighed.

Now Papa has left the *Pakistan Times,* and hates it, his retirement. It leaves him lying in a bed surrounded by telephones that will not ring, and he hates such active suspension. There is nothing of my mother left in his house now, of course, and our visits seem to cause him increasing unease, reminding him of some other thing that he once knew, a memory international. He still has Shahida, but "I am alone, alone!" he groaned to me when I last went to see him in Islamabad. I pointed out to him that in the last fifty years he had had two wives, six children, eleven grandchildren, and now also had a brand-new daughter. "And that's only your official record!" I added, jauntily. But Pip did not want to leave his mood of darkening cloud. "I have done nothing with my life!" he cried, "I have written nothing!" I told him that he had all the time to make a bigning now and write *Boys Will Be Boys*—a wonderful book, I knew. He shook him mane and sighed, gazing down upon his vacant fingers. "What would I say," he wondered to himself instead of me, "and what could I just not?" Then, "For, Sara, I have done some terrible things!" "Such as, Papa?" I asked gently, sad at this confession, coming latter-day. I was relieved when he became professional again about the business of his news. "If God has been merciful enough to keep my secrets," retorted Pip, "should I be so ungrateful as to tell them to you?" No, my dear, my dear, I thought to myself, protect my being in the end and keep some information from me. That night I knew I should not visit him again if I wished to spare his soul chagrin, and so I practiced at its utterance, good-bye, and then good-bye.

Years ago, shortly after Mamma died, Tillat and I both noticed and wondered at Papa's latest nervous quirk. He had begun to use his index finger as a pen, making it in constant scribbles write on each surface it could find. He did not seem aware of this new habit, but whether he was eating at the table or ensconced in his old green chair, Papa's finger moved on in ghostly hieroglyphics, as though to abjure the idiosyncrasy of speech. "But what is he writing?" Tillat marveled. "It must be something Urdu, for he's moving from right to left." I told her I was sure that she had misread the event, that his finger moved with the pattern of the fabric, left to right. "Are you certain?" she answered, disbelievingly, "I could swear that it looked like Urdu." But as we whispered on in the half-light, we both felt cognizant of a more pressing issue: in a room we could not see, a hand was still awake. It sought the secrecy of surface in the dark, and its finger was writing, writing.

Communal Violence and Literature

ISMAT CHUGHTAI

The flood of communal violence came and went with
all its evils, but it left a pile of living, dead and gasping corpses
in its wake. It wasn't only that the country was split in two—
bodies and minds were also divided. Moral beliefs were tossed
aside and humanity was in shreds. Government officers and
clerks along with their chairs, pens and inkpots, were distributed like the spoils of war. And whatever remained after this
division was laid to waste by the benevolent hands of communal violence. Those whose bodies were whole had hearts that
were splintered. Families were torn apart. One brother was
allotted to Hindustan, the other to Pakistan; the mother was in
Hindustan, her offspring were in Pakistan; the husband was in
Hindustan, his wife was in Pakistan. The bonds of human relationship were in tatters, and in the end many souls remained
behind in Hindustan while their bodies started off for
Pakistan.

Communal violence and freedom became so muddled that
it was difficult to distinguish between the two. After that, anyone who obtained a measure of freedom discovered violence
came alongside. The storm struck without any warning, so people couldn't even gather their belongings. When things cooled
down a bit people collected themselves and had a chance to
observe what was going on around them.

With every aspect of life disrupted by this earth-shaking event, how could poets and writers possibly sit by without saying a word? How could literature, which has close ties with life, avoid getting its shirt-front wet when life was drenched in blood? Forgetting the struggles of love and separation, people concentrated on saving their skin and bones. Like the followers of Satan, they went beyond the conventional styles of romance. Caravans of refugees put Farhad's wandering in the desert to shame, and even the ghazal, regarded as the beloved of feudal aristocracy, forgot its gambols and, escaping from the alley of the adored one, began drifting among the burning bazaars, pillaged houses and heaps of crushed humanity. There was no other recourse. After all, *"gham-e janaan"* had to be transformed one day into *"gham-e dauraan"*.

As soon as the writers and poets had a moment to breathe, they turned towards their objective. A variety of viewpoints and sentiments, some progressive, some reactionary, and still others that were neither of these but some mysterious entity in the middle, could be observed. Some writers, armed with plaster and mortar, threw themselves headlong into laying this mortar and whitewashing.

Walls that had crumbled were raised again, leaking roofs were repaired, demolished halls were given a new lease of life—the individuals doing this were motivated by a creative literary purpose. Foremost among them were writers born under the canopy of foreign rule who had long since become disillusioned with it and, now disgruntled, were looking forward to its departure from their country. The moment they saw the white-skinned pirates leaving Hindustan they danced about and gamboled, clapping their hands like little children. They were so intoxicated with the notion of freedom that they felt no shame or embarrassment in jumping about excitedly on the streets. And anyway, who had time to be embarrassed? The Union Jack was slipping while the *tiranga* was being raised high. The nationalists allowed their thoughts to soar. Just as the four-anna wallahs in cinema halls whistle loudly and express their delight at the appearance of the hero mounted on his steed, so these intoxicated lovers of freedom danced and celebrated in the streets when they saw the heroic *tiranga* soaring in the sky.

"*Dance joyfully, sing songs of mirth,*" Prem Dhawan sang.

"*Advance, because the time is for singing and celebration; arise, it is the arrival of spring,*" Josh Sahib roared.

"*The sun has come out with such pride today/Himalaya's lofty peaks are glittering,*" Jazbi proclaimed emotionally. Jazbi said excitedly:

Sing, o Ganga,
Move lightly, breeze of the garden.
Shimmer joyously, Himal
For the mountains and valleys are dancing.
And statues of Ajanta,
Sing on, sing on!

"*Free, free, Hindustan is free,*" Jaan Nisar Akhtar said rapturously.

My Delhi, my beloved Delhi.
No longer the whore of tyrannical emperors,
No longer the slave-girl of feudal lords,
The market of the foreign capitalists.
But the centre of our hopes, the realization of our dreams.
The image of our desires.

"*I see a radiance on your face today...*" Jafri declared.

But 15th August came and went, leaving behind embarrassed, whimpering and teary-eyed masses. The hearts that had been singing were hushed, the dancing feet were stilled. Those who continued to dance had no idea what beat or melody they were dancing to. Disappointed hearts began to understand. Suddenly it became clear that they had been handed a tinned moon with plating so brittle that it didn't last for more than two days. What they had welcomed as the morn of truth was just a firecracker whose temporary brightness had seduced

naive hearts into singing for joy. The ones who departed went
so adroitly that they took only the body and left the soul behind. What a tragedy that they divided freedom into two parts
and handed them to the people, saying "Pakistan is for the
Pakistanis and Hindustan is for the Hindustanis." But when
the accounts were settled it became clear that the bigwigs of
Hindustan and Pakistan got everything while those who had
been empty-handed before Partition remained empty-handed.
As the saying goes, a blind man distributing *rewaries* kept dol-
ing them out to his kinsmen. So Josh Sahib spoke angrily:

> *This measuring, this cutting, this wanton devastation*
> *The drowning of the swimmers, the helplessness of the*
> > *fighters,*
>
> *What shall we call autumn if this is spring?*

And Sardar Jafri gnashed his teeth and proclaimed furiously:

> *From whose forehead has the ink of slavery been wiped*
> > *off?*
>
> *The anguish of bondage torments my heart still*
> *There is the same sadness on the face of Mother India,*
> *Daggers are free to plunge into bosoms,*
> *Death is free to drift upon corpses.*

And Majaz said quietly:

> *All these whose hands are dripping with blood,*
> *They were the very messiahs, the Khizrs.*

From across the border Ahmed Nadeem Qasmi informed us
that all was not well there either:

> *Pieces of bread weighed against snippets of flesh*
> *In shops decorated with honour,*
> *After the appetite is satiated,*
> *The taste of blood dances upon the tongue.*

And Majrooh said irately:

> *Now it is they who had once endured the pain of captivity*
> *Who bequeath the pain of captivity.*

And Akhtar said tearfully:

I was happy that my country had been freed.

But he soon found out that

The flower lost its colour the moment it was touched,
The garland had yet to be braided when it came undone
The goblet hadn't touched the lips when it was shattered,
It's not my dreams that have been looted and pillaged, it
                                                    is me.

In other words, there were protests everywhere. But before a demand for an explanation could gain strength, communal riots burst upon the scene with a blast. Clearly, dealing with the violence became more important than the clamour for rights. Most of the progressive writers in Hindustan and Pakistan turned their attention to this issue and, helped by other progressive elements, began their work in earnest. The force of the pen thwarted the attacks of the knife and dagger. Although the reactionaries sided with the dagger and knife, it was the progressive elements that finally won. This was a time when the value of life was equivalent to a fistful of sand. The helpless victims had been unleashed in the field; every demand was met by adding fuel to the blaze of communal violence. The organizers were standing with their backs turned; the reformers of the nation were dozing somewhere out of sight. This was the moment when writers provided ammunition in the form of plays, sketches, stories and poems, scattering them everywhere. Ahmed Abbas scribbled his play, *Main Kaun Hun?* (Who Am I?) in ninety minutes, rehearsed it, and that same evening arranged performances in several parts of the city. Abbas did not have time to consider the fact that his haste might compromise his art, that it might belittle the power of his pen, that a writer's greatness might be diminished. If he had thought about all this he might have turned *Main Kaun Hun?* into great art, but then it couldn't have doused the fire blazing at this time. This burning world needs dousing more than it needs works of art.

Around this time Krishan Chander set up a veritable fortification and sent an army of *afsaanas*, stories and sketches into the field.The speed with which the riots spread was matched by the speed with which Krishan's *afsaanas* were circulated through magazines in both Hindustan and Pakistan. Intentionally or unintentionally, this bombardment occurred in such a way that no other example can be found anywhere in the world, where one writer produced so much material in such a short period of time, and his prescription truly proved beneficial. Whatever Krishan Chander wrote, he wrote dispassionately, wittingly and, perhaps, under pressure. It may not have come naturally to him and may appear affected, but he wrote because he felt he had to, because the situation called for it.

This was the time when both fact ons were already sparring with each other. A count hadn't been done yet to determine which side had eliminated more adversaries. If the Muslims had taken out a procession of two thousand naked women, the Hindus had taken one out with four thousand. The Muslims six thousand. The Hindus eight thousand. Eight thousand, sixteen thousand, thirty-two thousand, one hundred thousand. If there had been someone clever among them, he would have done a count and then announced which party's stalwarts had emerged victorious. But the fact is, every victor looked vanquished, everyone's head was lowered in remorse.

Whatever Krishan Chander, Ahmed Abbas, Sardar Jafri, Ahmed Nadeem Qasmi, Upendar Nath Ashk, Sahir Ludhianvi, Hajira Masroor and others of this family have written under the circumstances, has been denied its place as literature by Aziz Ahmed, Hasan Askari and M. Aslam. They claim that these [progressive] writers have weighed everything on a scale and given each savage an equal share; they think that in actuality only Hindus and Sikhs committed atrocities. I don't know on what grounds they make this claim. Perhaps they have been

supplied their figures by the brutes themselves, because anyone with any sense at all knows that both factions have committed atrocities and each side has attempted to outdo the other.
In their opinion only a one-sided picture can clearly portray
the events that took place. For example, they think Krishan
Chander should only have written about what he saw with his
own eyes. Just what would have happened had he done so? At
the time Krishan Chander wrote his *afsaanas*, his house had
been turned into a camp for refugees. Seeing the terrible condition of those who had fled from western Punjab, observing
the effects of their mental and physical abuse, who knows what
anger might have welled up in Krishan's heart against the
Muslims? Who knows what blinding curtain might not have
covered his eyes that otherwise only discerned the truth as he
sat among his near and dear ones? But what emotion and what
strength made him throw off that blindfold and look beyond?
How many times, afraid that he was becoming biased, must
he have had to escape from his environment so that, away
from the searing sighs of these sorrowful victims, he could
draw the other side of the picture, using only his creative vision? Searching carefully and diligently, he selected and produced images that would have the same weight on the scales
when they were exhibited. And during this time, anyone who
loved his country would have done just that. On one side of
the scale he put eyewitness accounts and on the other, pic-
tures called forth from his imagination. If it had been anyone
else he would have cheated. Or, like M. Aslam, he would have
taken only one side of the scale into account. Or, as Askari
Sahib suggests, he may not have called a tyrant a tyrant, nor
condemned tyranny and he may not have made an effort to
combat evil. He would have written a few silly jokes and waited
for that innate goodness (that supposedly accompanies base-
ness in every individual) to surface and, labelling it an immor-
tal literary creation, he would then have expected apprecia-
tion and approval. In my opinion, even if Krishan Chander
throttled literature, trampled on the refined elements of art and

created phony writing, he certainly did not remain unaware of his duty. He engaged in propaganda and became a rectifier of wrong. At a time when we needed a leader more urgently than we needed an artist, he did what was necessary, what was proper. In the eyes of Hasan Askari, Krishan might be a re-forming idiot, perhaps because Askari himself was seduced by just such a reformer's role. But we have got nothing to do with Hasan Askari's values. We have immutable values before us. We will keep our sights on them.

Despite all this, whatever Krishan Chander and others wrote about the communal violence is not at all inferior by literary standards. The style, plot and imaginative quality of *Hum Vahshi Hain* (We Are Savages) are superior to all of Krishan Chander's earlier collections. The passion, the tenderness which wasn't apparent in *Yahaan ke Nazaare* (The Views Here) nor in *Shikast* (Defeat) and which, in fact, can be seen in no other work except *An Daata* (Master), are present here. The recent fiery passion that has become a part of Krishan's work is due in great part to the fact that now there is a special commitment in his work, a purpose, a resolve and its subsequent realiza-tion. And this is what elevates his writing to such heights.

The second type of people are those who beat their chests and lament for their respective communities, thus encourag-ing and extolling the forces of factionalism. Toadies of feudal-ism and capitalism, they are opportunists and enemies of the people. They spend every last ounce of their energy to protect the spoils of war that fell into their hands when the country was divided. They believe that the common people are out to forcibly snatch their loot, so they are trying to distract them by staging communal riots. They have been trained by the British and are their true heirs. In the past, whenever the Hindustanis expressed a desire to be free, these people immediately insti-gated riots. Now that the British have left (physically), these new rulers fear that this freedom-only-in-name will be seen for what it is. There is no other recourse for them but to hide behind religious differences and split the country in two.

Besides, as the saying goes, we are flogging a dead horse. In other words, first the country is divided and then to make matters worse, there are communal riots. Continual dissension must be created to keep this division alive.

Keeping these very considerations in mind, M. Aslam wrote his *Raqs-e Iblis* (The Dance of Satan). Except for its reactionary sentiments, this novel has nothing to offer. It is neither interesting nor stimulating. The narrative style is puerile and flat. Because not a single episode, from start to finish, has been presented in a realistic, effective manner, there is little or no verisimilitude in the entire novel. The characters are stereotyped and crudely delineated. Two rather silly male characters engage in a conversation in stilted, broken language about this rumour and that, speaking so inanely that after a while one feels no desire to continue reading. The novel's hero, Mehbub Elahi, has fled from East Punjab after losing everything, including his bride who was kidnapped the day after he married her. Just before he leaves he buries his mother with his own hands. In spite of all that he has suffered he carries on quite pleasantly about clean beds, *baaqarkhaanis* and sugar. But in the end, when his kidnapped wife, assaulting everyone along the way like the heroine from *The Stunt Queen*, returns to him completely unharmed and still a virgin, a tirade of anger and invectives is let loose against seven generations of the other group.

If someone with a more forceful pen than M. Aslam had written a novel from this point of view, it would indeed have been a dangerous work. However, as things stand, there's no such fear. But, let's forget the novel. What is more important is the preface, the product of Hasan Askari's pen. After reading just the first page it is clear what the narrative contains and how crudely it is presented. With the exception of M. Aslam, Hasan Askari, and perhaps Aziz Ahmed, no other critic in Pakistan, progressive or otherwise, has praised *Raqs-e Iblis*. Apparently the reactionary front is not very strong in either Hindustan or Pakistan.

As a counterpoint to M. Aslam's thrust, Ramanand Sagar wrote a novel, *Aur Insaan Mar Gaya* (And Humanity Died). I read both these novels at about the same time. Technique aside, the two novels are very similar in terms of subject matter and point of view. Although Ramanand Sagar was not a progressive writer, he was not a reactionary either. Placing him in the same category as M. Aslam I feel as if I, too, am standing alongside them. This is because I have always regarded Ramanand as a member of my own family and it pains me to see him sharing M. Aslam's views.

In *Raqs-e Iblis* M. Aslam has written about the atrocities committed by the Hindus and Sikhs against the Muslims.

In *Aur Insaan Mar Gaya* Ramanand Sagar has written about the atrocities committed by the Muslims against Hindus and Sikhs.

M. Aslam has a Sikh who risks his own life in order to save Muslims.

Ramanand Sagar also manages to find a Muslim maulana to perform a similar service for him.

M. Aslam's heroine is kidnapped by Sikhs and Ramanand's is seized by Muslims.

At this point, however, M. Aslam offers greater evidence of his progressivism. When his heroine, Khursheed, returns to Pakistan, her husband accepts her without asking any questions. On the other hand, when Ramanand Sagar's heroine returns, ravaged and ruined, she is so disheartened by the stupid hero's indifference that she commits suicide. Ramanand Sagar seems reluctant to support a fallen woman.

In M. Aslam's narrative the ending is optimistic; the future, as he sees it, is bright. In Ramanand's story there is only despair, a hopelessness that seems to reach new heights of silliness.

M. Aslam's characters, those that are left intact, start a new life.

Ramanand's commit moral and physical suicide, they go mad and behave savagely, hoping thus to attract the reader's sympathy.

The preface to *Aur Insaan Mar Gaya* has been written by Ahmed Abbas, who has done everything possible to outdo Hasán Askari in his reactionism. For instance, while Askari Sahib remarks that *Raqs-e Iblis* is truly creative and constructive literature, Ahmed Abbas says he saw a lone star in the darkness and it was Ramanand Sagar. And the fact that he (Ramanand) thinks that humanity is dead is the very proof that humanity is indeed not dead. I don't know what kind of logic this is. Maybe Ramanand Sagar and Ahmed Abbas alone have grasped that "pessimism" *is* in reality "optimism". When Ramanand Sagar killed every human being and every animal in his novel, Abbas was convinced that "death" is, in reality, "life" and everything else is just plain nonsense.

Askari Sahib says that the people actually responsible for communal violence are the Sikhs and the Hindus; the poor Muslims only committed atrocities now and then to defend themselves. Ahmed Abbas feels that ordinary people started the riots, that they are solely responsible for all the violence and that they slit each other's throats just for the fun of it. In saying this he ignores completely the effect of years and years of foreign rule and colonialism. He probably believes that it was these very people who demanded Pakistan and got it.

Such Hindustanis and Pakistanis wish to shield with their writing that particular class which, driven by a desire for personal gain, in fact perpetrated and was the real progenitor of the Partition and its ensuing violence. This class is not particular to any one country, but rather, except for a few nations, is found everywhere on earth. It commits such acts and looks for similar justifications.

However, we shouldn't be fearful nor should we lose hope. Such writing has rarely been taken seriously or applauded by the general public. It's possible that they may be swayed momentarily, but these tabors and kettledrums cannot keep the public distracted for long.

However, there are others who form links between constructive and destructive literature in this chain. Among them is the one represented in Mumtaz Shirin's short story, "Bharat Mata." The gist of the story is that first Mother India is cut up into many parts—which is all right—and she feels some pain; then she is convinced that whatever has happened is for the best. By personifying Hindustan as a mother, Mumtaz Shirin has flung the word "mother" face down into slime. Is there a mother anywhere whose child is torn in two and she claps her hands joyfully, exclaiming, "Ahha, ahha! Now there are two, and both are my sons." This analogy is crude and frightening. I respectfully submit that if the Honoured Lady is a mother herself, then it is very odd indeed that she should present such a ridiculous view regarding children. And if she's not burdened with being a mother herself, she's still a woman, and a woman can never tolerate a mockery of the mother-child relationship nor deliberately attack it. Even without this analogy, her proposition that if something is split in two it will thrive better, sounds odd. Does this mean that if left whole it will stop growing? The Respected Lady is harbouring a grave misconception. It's possible that division will momentarily staunch the flow of the rapids, but if by some chance the two parts come together at some point, no barrier or forethought will be able to stem the ensuing deluge. What will happen if the courage and resolve weakened by the division were restored? She didn't think this through. But no, I'm mistaken. She has indeed thought it through carefully and is saying all this as part of a calculated programme. All the same, these tactics will prove ineffective in the end. Meanwhile her kind of literature is even more lethal than literature generally regarded as destructive. For the latter merely aims at causing disruption, while the former conspires to dig out the very roots of the tree and plant a new seed. Should such a seed ever take root, it will crush willpower by holding out false hopes and hollow promises.

I'm at a loss about what to do with [Saadat Hasan] Manto's *Siyah Haashiye* (Black Margins): should I catalogue it as a work of literature or should I find an entirely new classification for it? Manto is very fond of things that create an uproar and awaken with a start even those who are fast asleep. He thinks that if a man smeared with mud walks into a group of people all dressed in shining white, this will shock them; or if someone bursts into raucous laughter in a gathering of people weeping and wailing, this will make them stare at him in wonder. Well, that will impress everyone, he will be famous.

Usually this tactic pays off, and Manto has managed to receive a lot of applause, but the arrow has missed its mark this time. Surely *Siyah Haashiye* is neither a masterpiece nor a timeless marvel, but it's not garbage either. There are several pieces in this collection that move us to tears. But in his preface Muhammad Hasan Askari has done the collection a great injustice. He has misrepresented the contents by cloaking them in a garb suited to his own fancy. What does he mean by saying that Manto does not regard tyranny as tyranny? Does he think that he regards the tyrant as the beloved? I don't think Manto ever says such a thing. Whatever else he might do, Manto would never claim that evil people are creations of their own minds or that God has made them this way, or that social and political forces play no part in making them what they are. Askari Sahib believes that tyrants should not be opposed because they won't change. Is he suggesting that if someone hits you over the head with a club you should say, "Well, brother, let me have a few more blows?" Askari Sahib may possess such lofty sentiments, but no sane person can tolerate this sort of thing, certainly not Manto. Manto will use conciliatory tactics only so far; if a person persists in his aggression, he *will* resort to force. I don't know what pleasure Askari Sahib derives from mutilating Manto's point of view, but this ill serves Manto. Manto may be many things, but he cannot be bigoted, and won't be forced by anyone to become so; he won't approve of violence. A man whose heart melts at the plight of the most despicable whore scorned by the whole world, who can look into the heart of a human being as debased as a pimp, whose sensitive nose doesn't care for fragrance simply because it is characterized by affectation, sham and deception—Manto is not the sort of person who can fail to be affected by the sight of corpses. He is also not afraid of calling a tyrant a tyrant. Why would he hesitate to halt violence? We have been deceived. An attempt has been made to blur our vision. Manto's writing has been used as a tool to carry out some hidden agenda. His style is sometimes abstruse, he's used to presenting his ideas in a roundabout way, but I know that Manto was not laughing when he wrote *Siyah Haashiye,* nor did he write these tales to make people laugh. No matter how he is hoodwinked, Manto will never write reactionary literature.

This then is a glimpse into the kind of writing that was produced in the throes of the violence following Partition. What we have to see now is how much of it is going to survive and how much will be useful only as wrapping paper in an apothecary's shop. It is a mistake to say that this is merely riot-specific literature, and that as the violence dissipates, so will its importance and popularity. In one way or another, all literature is time-specific. Whatever Maulana Hali wrote during another tumultuous period of Indian history has survived as great literature. Likewise Gorki's writings will never be diminished in stature, although the revolution during which he wrote is long since over in his country. Every word that was written about the repugnant traditions of bondage is still highly valued today. And though the Spanish revolution is over, the greatness of *For Whom the Bell Tolls* endures.

So those who want to devalue the literature on communal violence by characterizing it as the product of a specific situation, and hence merely short-lived propaganda, are mostly individuals who couldn't produce anything of value themselves, or perhaps found it at odds with their own purpose. They are creating an impression that this literature is not significant in order to clear the field for themselves. The life and death of literature depend on its content as well as the talent of writers. It is total narrow-mindedness to say such literature is time-bound.

I don't mean to imply that every crisis will give rise to enduring works of literature. For example, a *sehra* written on the occasion of the wedding of a nawab sahib's darling dog, or a *marsiya* drafted by a school headmaster on a kalaktar sahib's transfer to another town will never be immortalized. To create great literature one needs a sensitive heart and specific goals, or, as the poet says:

There is no timeless subject in the world, Majrooh
Whatever I touched became eternal.

Ismat Chughtai (1915-1991), was the first Muslim woman in India to get degrees in BA and teaching. She established herself as a stalwart of Urdu fiction at a time when writing by and about women was both rare and tentative. She wrote novellas, novels, short stories, plays and essays. She produced and co-directed six films with her husband, and produced six more independently. She received a number of literary awards and was much acclaimed for her fiction writing.

This essay first appeared in Ismat Chughtai, My Friend, My Enemy: Essays, Reminiscences, Portraits, *translated by Tahira Naqvi. (Delhi: Kali for Women), 2001.*

Riots, Partition and Independence

MANIKUNTALA SEN

I did not have to wait long after 29 July. It was becoming clear that the country would be partitioned. General Wavell, the British Viceroy, was present in Delhi to deliver the parting kick before the empire came to an end. Power would be handed over. But to whom? Who would take over the responsibility, the Congress or the League? The British recommended that the country must be divided because Hindus and Muslims were two nations. Indian hearts did not beat in unison, Indians had, apparently, evolved as two distinct peoples who must now be separated. How terrible! I shuddered at the very thought.

Gandhiji was not prepared to aquiesce. He announced that the country would be partitioned over his dead body. I had no peace of mind either. In Barishal I had not witnessed Hindus and Muslims living like two separate peoples. If Barishal were to become a part of Pakistan, as this theory stated, then I would share Gandhiji's plight. My birthplace would become another country, and my heart would break. I knew my mother, brothers, sisters and the extended family would never leave their homes and come to Calcutta as refugees. That is why I could not reconcile myself to the two-nation theory. I was even more upset when I learnt that the Party had agreed to the Partition.

Before the transfer of independence Lord Wavell formed the Viceroy's Executive Council, and he himself became its president, with Nehru as its vice-president. The Muslim League was also called to participate but it refused to respond to the invitation. It preferred a direct confrontation to participation in the Council, and Jinnah Saheb gave a call for country-wide Direct Action. In Bengal the ministry in power was headed by Suhrawardy, the leader of the Muslim League.

On 16 August 1946, the government of Suhrawardy declared a holiday in Calcutta and the Muslim League gave a call to the Muslims to join in a procession. There was general apprehension that there would be trouble, and in various neighbourhoods Hindus prepared themselves for any eventuality. Our Party took the decision to accompany the procession so that if things started to get out of hand, party members would be able to intervene. But in the face of a deep-rooted conspiracy, the Party was bound to be ineffective. When the procession reached Dharamtala trouble began. Knives flashed and a number of people were injured in the clashes. Then there was widespread looting of all the shops. As the procession advanced along its route, the attacks and the looting increased. Those who were on the streets had come armed for action. The procession ultimately dispersed, and there was widespread rioting. The sounds of '*Lar ke lenge Pakistan*' and '*Allaho Akbar*' made the innocent city-dwellers panicky.

Hindus, Muslims and ordinary people did not want a riot. It was another matter for those who were involved in sectarian politics. At the call of the Muslim League, ordinary innocent people of Calcutta were butchered for three or four days. The homes of slum-dwellers, who only wanted to be left in peace to get on with their lives, were burnt; Hindus and Muslims who had lived side by side had to leave and settle in separate areas, for no fault of theirs. People lost their homes, many women lost their husbands and sons. I am not going to relate these stories. Those who were in Calcutta in August 1946 had witnessed what happened and had suffered similar experiences. In the face of the maddening fratricide the most precious things which Hindus and Muslims lost were trust and feelings of love and responsibility that they had for each other.

It was just seventeen or eighteen days ago that the historical strike of 29 July had witnessed the tying of rakhis between Hindus and Muslims on Rashid Ali Day, and before these events, Congress, League and the Communist Party's flags had flown side by side. It was no longer so. The result of years of effort by the women's organizations to unite Hindu and Muslim women lay shattered. And in the Chowringhee area, where the sahebs had not dared open their windows on 29 July, there was rejoicing. It seemed as if we were destined to receive this parting kick.

The Communist Party was in a real fix during this period. The unity of the workers and the people that had been forged with so much effort had disappeared completely. However, party workers and quite a few Hindu and Muslim families maintained amicable relations. This was like a silver lining in the dark clouds, which merits emphasis. On the night of 16 August, many workers and representatives of the Communist Party were stuck in various neighbourhoods. A number of Muslim workers likewise were held up at the tram workers' mess on Dover Lane. I came to hear of the strategy and surprising daring with which Hindu workers sent them home to the Park Circus area. Comrade Biren Roy was stuck in the slum areas of Kalabagan. In the middle of the night, Muslim workers of that place accompanied him to a safe area. Jolly Kaul and a few others had also been present in the peace procession of that day. But when the disturbances could not be staved off any further they went over to the Party commune in Khidderpore, not expecting that a riot would take place. Late that night Muslim comrades got them to a safe area. It was not possible to walk down the roads and so they were taken to safety through the many bylanes of the slums. Comrade Ajit Roy was a tenant in a flat belonging to a Gujarati Muslim who ran a leather business. Gita Mukherjee, Annada Shankar Bhattacharya and

Sukumar Gupta were holding a meeting nearby when the riot engulfed them, and they sought shelter with Ajit Roy. The Gujarati landlord protected them for three days, at great risk, although he had nothing to do with the Party. Comrades Bankim Mukherjee and Promode Dasgupta were at their commune, which was just a little further away. One day, sensing that things were not safe, they left and took shelter in Comrade Abdul Momin's house next door. Both the houses were on Central Avenue. The other tenants began to suspect that there were Hindus in the building and they wanted to enter the room and have a look. Momen Saheb managed to put them off for two days by saying his wife, Hasina, observed purdah. However, it grew impossible to put them off on the third day. In the evening the tenants threatened that they were going out to break their *roza*, but when they returned, Momen Saheb would have to dress up his wife in a burqa and bring her out of the room. They would then enter. They gave us just one hour of time.

Meanwhile Ajit Roy and the other comrades were in a similar situation. The local toughs were constantly pressurising the Gujarati gentleman to drive the Hindus out. Their claims were that the Hindus could observe what was going on and would have to be killed, or else they would reveal names and addresses as soon as they were released. They came and threatened that they would take steps once their *roza* was over. Ajit Roy and the others decided that they would leave Gita Mukherjee, who was ill, behind. The others would set out at the time of the breaking of *roza*, when the local *mastans* who assembled in front of the house would also disperse. If they were able to leap over the Medical College gate somehow, then they would be saved; or else everything might end just there. The Party meanwhile had been trying its utmost to send trucks with armed soldiers to rescue the comrades of both houses, who were aware of the plan and were waiting for the saviours to arrive. That day Indrajit Gupta and Mansur

Habibullah Saheb came in a military truck and saved the comrades at both houses in the nick of time.

There is no reason to relate this story in such detail other than to simply bring forth the indomitable courage, strength of mind and humanitarianism of Momin Saheb, Hasina and that Gujarati Muslim gentleman. The condition of the captives can easily be conjectured, but it is indeed more difficult for others to sense the tension borne by their rescuers day and night, every hour, every minute. Momin Saheb had to keep the smile on his face, his strength of mind intact and state repeatedly, 'There is no Hindu in my house.' The Gujarati gentleman suffered the same plight. After the rescue, Hasina and Momin Saheb had to leave their homes and come away to save their own lives. The neighbourhood toughs warned Momin Saheb, 'Don't come here again.'

Dr. Ghani of the Park Circus area had done the very same thing. This was the first time he got involved with us; he was not with the Party then. He was renowned in the neighbourhood as a generous doctor, caring for people, a benevolent friend to the slum-dwellers in particular. Today he is no more; but when the slum-dwellers queue up in front of the charitable institution established by him every morning, they probably still remember him. During the riots he would convey the Hindus, trapped in this neighbourhood, to Ballygunge at midnight. He had saved a family of dhobis living next to his house with great difficulty. A number of men who lived in the Park Circus area supported him, gave shelter to the Hindu families in their houses, and tried various ways to send them to safe neighbourhoods. I saw the same thing happen in Ballygunge. Many Muslim families were able to reach Park Circus with the assistance of Party workers or other people.

Relief centres for the families which had come from Park Circus and lost their homes, were started at Jashoda Mansion and the Kamala Girls' School. In both the places, men and women workers of that neighbourhood carried out relief work. One day, at the Kamala Girls' School, I met a Muslim family who were in hiding there. At night they were to be transferred to the Park Circus area. The plan was known to some but it caused no unusual concern because many people had been exchanged between neighbourhoods in this manner. Both Hindus and Muslims were involved, and in the midst of darkness, this little ray of light was the only thing that restored our faith in the basic goodness of humanity.

Side by side there were incidents that revealed the other side of the picture. Many Muslims used to come to the Gariahat Market from the villages to sell fish and vegetables. On the first day when the riots broke out, many of them had already returned to the safety of the villages in the afternoon. Amongst those present, some had been able to escape but others had been killed. The next day only a few villagers came to sell their wares; rioters were waiting at the station for them and many of the vendors were beaten up and killed. A few medical students who used to live in the house next to ours got hold of an old egg-seller. They started beating him with a makeshift weapon made of bones. The man came running to our doorstep, trying to escape his assailants. When I tried to open the door, the landlord's brother grabbed me from behind and stopped me from opening the door. Blows had split the egg-seller's head and blood was smeared on the walls. Then the young men dragged him aside and murdered him. The landlord's wife had fallen at her husband's feet and screamed, "Save him!" but he was unmoved. We remained mute witnesses to his death. The bloodstain on the wall remained for many days. It was horrible to look at; you got a queer feeling that the man might start speaking from somewhere.

We undertook relief work at Jashoda Mansion, where a relief centre for the families which had been rescued had been started. On one side there were facilities for women and children, on the other for men. One of the women went mad, brooding over her dead husband. All she knew was that her husband had not been able to get out of a room which had caught fire. We kept that woman tied up in a veranda on the fourth floor. The Rashbehari tramline was in front. There was no disturbance or excitement on the roads. This was probably the fourth day of the riot; there were hardly any Muslims left in the Ballygunge area. Suddenly, we saw that a gentleman and his wife, who was carrying a child in her arms, were being dragged out from a tram. The man was a Muslim. Later I learnt that they had come from Howrah and were not aware of the riot. Within minutes, about five hundred people had assembled on the road, many holding bamboo poles. I wondered why it took so many people and such a huge number of sticks to beat one single person to death! The wife fell at every person's feet, crying, begging for her husband's life. I noticed some people taking her away and hiding her in a shop.

In the meantime, the woman who was insane with grief wanted to commit suicide, jumping down from the fourth floor. A few of us sat with her, holding her to keep her steady. When I saw that terrible sight on the road, I thought is there really any difference between this woman and that one on the road? Both were wives who were dependent on their husbands, both were mothers, both wanted to die. What favour were we doing them by keeping them alive? Were those who killed their husbands human?

I will not write any more about the riots. Nor is it possible to describe such disgraceful conduct. I was under the impression that women could not be a party to violence. But thanks to what I saw in the Ballygunge area, I had to abandon this illusion. I will not mention the name of the road I was walking down one day on my way to the Rashbehari tramline from Fern Road. I noticed a slight stir. From the top floor of the houses, women were throwing stout sticks down into the hands of the men standing below. I wondered what the problem was. It seemed that the Muslims were coming, and I assumed that they were coming to attack in a huge group. I was slightly scared too as I was on the road. Then I was shocked to hear that all this excitement in the neighbourhood was about a person wearing a lungi. Was he or wasn't he a Muslim? Later when people found out who he was, they were reassured. I thought of something else. A few hundred brave people had come to put an end to this single individual. Why were the women handing down lathis to their husbands and sons instead of trying to stop them? Why does the madness engendered by the riots bring a person to such depths? Why does it wipe out the natural softness of a woman's heart? Why was this happenng in our area? Had we inquired around we would probably have come to learn that the picture was the same in the Muslim areas. This is probably what happens when the animal instincts of a person are aroused. Humanity survives simply because there are exceptions coexisting side by side.

The riots continued. The police had started patrolling the streets. Had this been done earlier, the situation could have been kept under control, but this is what happens when politics gets the upper hand. Buses and trams ran again, and people walked down the streets as they used to. We too started going to the office of the mahila samiti in Bowbazar. One day, in the afternoon, I visited the house of a Muslim couple who were friends of the Party and lived in the Park Circus area. Their names were Ismail Saheb and Roshanara. Kamala and I and many other communists would often go to their house. Attractive, blessed with good taste, the couple was also very hospitable, and we could never leave without eating a meal with them. Just before Ismail Saheb was about to leave for work, I took my leave and, boarding a Number 10 bus, went to the samiti office. Everything seemed normal. But as soon as I got down at the Bowbazar crossing, I felt that the atmosphere was tense. As I walked down the road, I saw blood-stained bodies lying about. I could not make out what was happening and walked as quickly as I could to our office. As soon as I got upstairs the others exclaimed, "How did you get here? There has been a terrible riot." My heart skipped a few beats. Could Ismail Saheb be in danger? Besides, what if there was a riot in Barishal! I stood on the veranda and witnessed the most horrible scenes. A bullock-cart was going down the road without its driver. He had been killed and left inside the cart. The butchers in the meat shops had come out brandishing their heavy cleavers. We did not know whether they were Hindus or Muslims. The road itself seemed to have turned into a butcher's shop amidst the screams and terrifying cries. A man stood behind me. His family ran a tea business in another room in the building. Suddenly becoming very excited, he started screaming, trying to point out where the Muslims were hiding. I could not stand it any more. I rebuked him sharply, saying, "Do you know what the outcome of this will be? If a single Muslim is killed here the life of a Hindu in East Bengal will also be endangered. My mother, brother and sister are Hindus; they live in East Bengal. Remember, if anything happens to any of them I will hold you responsible. Besides, if you instigate murderous tendencies here, I will set the police on you." The man seemed to shrivel up. I knew how ridiculous the threat of handing someone over to the police was! I could see for myself that the police were coming over from Lalbazar not to stop the riots, but to pick up the dead bodies that were lying on the road. The situation , however, improved a little by evening and I was able to go home by bus.

I now heard of the riots in Barishal. Here, too, it was the same story. The steamer from Dhaka reached the Barishal river jetty at midnight. The rioters lay in wait, ready to ambush. They had planned that just as the steamer's siren sounded, they would launch an attack on the disembarking passengers. And this is just what they did. A few Muslims saved my younger brother in the most surprising manner. My brother had a restaurant named Ruchira, because of which he was popular with both Hindu and Muslim patrons. That day, just after 9 pm, a few Muslim men who were to join the rioters some time later, came and started warning him repeatedly, "Why have you left the restaurant open till so late? Now you must go home." When Satu refused to get up in spite of repeated reminders, they summoned a rickshaw and practically forced him to get on it. They said, "The times are bad. Do not stay out till so late." They warned the rickshaw-wallah, "You must drive fast, and reach him home quickly." Satu recalled later that the siren of the steamer from Dhaka had sounded after the rickshaw had covered half the distance. Immediately the signal reached all the outposts. There were sounds of anguish and terror everywhere, and flames lit up the horizon.

The next day, about three hundred Hindu villagers took shelter in our house, where in the meantime many young Muslim men set up an anti-riot camp. I was to hear about this later in Barishal. When the riots stopped, the Hindu and Muslim families left the camps and slowly began returning to their respective neighbourhoods. The camp at Jashoda Mansion in Ballygunge, Calcutta, had gradually been wound up in this manner.

During the riots, Noakhali and Comilla had been the worst affected among the districts of East Bengal. Renu, Kamala and a few others went to Hainchar in Noakhali where the situation was dreadful. They carried out some relief work and returned In the meantime, Gandhiji had opened a camp in Noakhali and begun a *padyatra*. I was sent to Chandpur where a centre for women had been started, and Abani Lahiri's wife, Maya, accompanied us. The centre had been opened with government aid by a mission. Along with the AIWC women, we too were to share the responsibility for running the centre, which is why Maya Lahiri and I had come as quickly as we could. We found a place to stay next to the maternity centre, and the young male cadres also arranged for a cook. We started to work, and within a few days we were able to manage things properly.

One evening, we heard that Ashoka Gupta of the AIWC, Renuka Roy, Shri and Shrimati P.K.Roy (the grandparents of Renuka Roy) and some others had met with an accident some distance from Chandpur. The jeep had turned over, Renuka Roy and her grandmother had fallen under it and both had been injured severely, saved from death only because there was silt underneath. We brought two beds from the maternity centre and various other things needed for nursing, which we arranged in a room. The patients came with mud smeared all over their bodies and with broken ribs. I was their nurse for three days. In the morning and in the evening, Ashoka Gupta would come to help. During the afternoon or at night I was the one who looked after the patients. Renuka Roy was quite pleased with me because of this and was also slightly surpris ed at the thought that Communist women were also capable of serving the Congress in this manner! That is why, on a cer- tain night, she whispered into my ear, "Mani, why did you turn into a Communist?" I said, "We can talk later, it is mid- night now, try to get some sleep." She said, "But you must not leave", and holding my hand for a while, she fell asleep. What could I have done? The women patients returned to Calcutta after a few days and I went back to my own work.

I recall a somewhat unusual incident. A young woman who had taken shelter in our home was friendly with a young Mus- lim man, a friend of her elder brother. Apparently it was all fixed up that she would marry him, and her dada did not dis- approve either. She related the story to us and asked us to write to him to come and take her away. This in itself was quite a simple matter, but I was disgusted with the resulting clamour. Some members of the religious institution with which we were working, said, "Cut the girl into pieces and throw them into the river." I was shocked to find that sanyasis wear- ing saffron, who claimed to have given their lives in the serv- ice of the people, could be so communal.

In the meantime, we were having a difficult time trying to take care of the young woman. Maya and I both tried to tell her: come with us to Calcutta, we shall teach you how to read and write and then you can marry anyone. But she refused to be convinced. As far as I remember, her father or brother came and took her away. She had been widowed at a very young age and lived with her brother's family. Would any Hindu marry a young widow readily? Under such circumstances, if she found a respectable husband and a new family for herself, how could anyone object? How could this threaten society and bring about its collapse? If this was what Hindu society was like, how dare we call others communal?

Phulrenu Guha came to meet me. She kept asking me repeatedly to return to Calcutta. The way she kept insisting made me realize that something untoward had happened at our home in Fern Road. The house was no longer a commune. Before I left I had made arrangements for my sick sister, her husband and their two sons and two daughters to stay there. I did not know that my sister was so ill that she would die. The other members of my family had come with her, as I had planned, and she died on the ninth day. Phulrenu had heard this news before she left Calcutta and therefore had done her utmost to persuade me to go home. I left and Maya Lahiri stayed on.

Meanwhile, independence was imminent. Gandhiji was in Noakhali. He had been trying to unite Hindus and Muslims all over again so that the country would not be divided. But none of the Congress factions were prepared to wait any longer. On the one hand there were Jinnah's threats, on the other Mountbatten Saheb came with his plans of Partition in March 1947. From March till 13 August, there was a round of conferences on the transfer of power with leaders like Nehru and Patel. Gandhiji stayed away from all these discussions. He had not wanted Partition; yet he took no action to avert it. I have a feeling that the country would never have been divided if he had opposed it even more strongly. Meanwhile the fire lit by the countrywide conflagration burned on. The riots took a disastrous turn in Patna and in the Punjab.

Ultimately, the leaders decided to partition India, abandoning all efforts to prevent it. The areas that were to be incorporated on either side were also decided upon broadly. The only reward we received in trying to wash the wounds of the riots between August 1946 and August 1947 was a country, a country split in two, and some heartrending tears. Still we celebrated. The country might have been divided and broken into pieces, but independence had come ultimately. This time the sahebs would surely go back to Britain. The independence that was long awaited was declared on the midnight of 14 August. Calcutta was dressed up in garlands of lights and the voice of Jawaharlal sounded on the radio.

I cannot help but mention Suhrawardy's doings prior to independence. Gandhiji was then residing in a camp he had set up in the much devastated Beliaghata area. He addressed prayer meetings every day, calling for unity. He made appeals to the people to surrender their arms, and many people did so at his request. But who was that man standing behind the Mahatma? It was none other than the notorious Suhrawardy Saheb who had been the commander of the Direct Action. He appeared like a perfectly innocent cat, sitting with his tail rolled up, as if he was a soft, gentle domestic pet, such was the hypocritical expression on his face. He was mortally afraid that if he did not take shelter amongst the volunteers for peace set up by Gandhiji, he would not be safe. As I watched him, I burned with indignation.

I felt frustrated that Suhrawardy got what he had wanted. And what did Gandhiji get? The father of the nation no longer remained its leader when India was actually divided into two. But even that was not able to save him. Ultimately, he too had to give up his life, struck down by a fatal shot from a Hindu in a prayer meeting. Gandhiji's offence was that he had struggled to maintain communal harmony. Strangely, the leaders of the country seemed to feel that their duty was over by simply sending the accused to the gallows. There was not even an inquiry; lest the cat come out of the bag. The fear has been reborn today as the tentacles of communalism are spreading under the leadership of the RSS and the Jana Sangh. Those untouchables whom Gandhiji had wanted to uplift from the mire of hatred and ignominy, and whom he had called the children of God (Harijan), are being burnt to death. Armed groups are indiscriminately murdering women and children in different parts of the country. Religious bigotry, linguistic feuds and communalism are looming larger, trying to break up India into a thousand fragments. These people no longer take pride in calling themselves Indians. What is the point of paying respect to martyrs on Gandhiji's death anniversary by observing silence for two minutes? What is the point of working at the charkha and singing *Ramdhuns* through the night, burying Gandhiji's ideals in futile rituals?

Manikuntala Sen was a prominent figure on the political stage of Bengal between the 1940s and 1960s. Born in 1910 into a conservative upper caste, middle-class family, she broke free of familial and social bonds to reach out to a cause. Beginning her political journey as a college student, she became a member of the Communist Party and rose to become the deputy leader of the Opposition in the West Bengal Legislative Assembly.

Excerpted from Manikuntala Sen, In Search of Freedom: An Unfinished Journey (*Calcutta: Stree*), *2001.*

Partition: Streams of Refugees

MANIKUNTALA SEN

ndependence came, we know, with the partition of the country, and across the border of a divided Bengal came groups of displaced refugees who had lost everything; their slogan of '*Amra kara? Bastuhara'* ('Who are we? Refugees who have lost our homes and everything else too') rising to the skies. Today, after thiry-five years, most of them have settled down, merging their lives with those of people everywhere in India, and certainly with the inhabitants of West Bengal. What colossal sufferings did those cataclysmic days bring! Many first took shelter in the houses of relatives, others squatted on the platforms of Sealdah, and finally went to the camps. Maybe the new government was incapable of coping with the millions who had poured in, but there was no mistaking the fact that their reception was like that of unwanted people. People try to survive by any means. They will even clear jungles to create space for themselves, as the history of mankind tells us. Those who did not wish to stay in the refugee camps put up by the government at Sealdah, Dhubulia and Ranaghat for these hordes of destitutes, gradually started to set up shelters for themselves on the northern, southern and eastern outskirts of Calcutta. There was not an empty house or an empty space left. The refugees started putting up their little huts and cottages, establishing their little colonies, clearing jungles and reclaiming marshy lands. Those who had managed to bring some money with them used it to build houses. However, simply possessing a house did not guarantee an income or ensure that they had enough to live on. Refugees built many *pakka* or permanent structures with their own resources on land that they had simply appropriated. These areas came to be known as squatters' colonies because they had been forcibly occupied, and periodically the government would try to evict them. To the government the legality of the possession was more important than the survival of the people. The law that settlements could not be built by reclaiming marshy lands that belonged to others, was enforced.

But the government was unable to remove refugees who had occupied these areas for sheer survival. A slogan that had been made popular by the peasants in the Tebhaga movement was, *'Jan debo to dhan debo na'* (I'd rather give up my life than my grain), and it was transformend to *'Jan debo to ghar debo na'* (I'd rather give up my life than my home). Each time the police demolished the huts and houses the refugees rebuilt them. Political leaders who had given their assent to the division of the country and had replaced the British rulers now tried to beat the hapless refugees into submission. But the government could not evade its responsibility for providing shelter to the refugees. Finally the Congress government, trying to crush the refugee movement, accepted defeat, just as earlier the Suhrawardy government had to yield on the issue of Tebhaga. Those who had been beaten up as 'unwanted' by the government regarded the Congress government as an unwanted entity too. It was the Communist Party that stood by the side of this vast, numerous, homeless and hapless multitude and created a network of organizations to administer to its needs. Organizations were built and the grievances of refugees were placed before the government. There were fierce struggles, on some occasions there were compromises. Eventually the squatter colonies received some recognition. Only those who had worked with such organizations were aware of the tears, the bloodshed and the many humiliations that lay beneath the surface of the lives of the refugees. I was witness to the horrors of the camps set up by the government. There was, of course, no easy solution to the problem. It was indeed a very difficult job to provide family-based rehabilitation to millions of people. As I toured the camps, I saw how camp life lowered the people's sense of self-respect. All were from East Bengal, and I could empathise keenly with their grief and suffering. It would prey on my mind constantly. At every camp people would show me the terribly poor quality of the clothes and the rice they received. I used to lobby the government on their behalf. To the refugees I would say that there was no point in protesting about the quality of rice and the clothes that had been given as dole. You should demand your right to work and accept the rice and the clothes only in exchange for such rights. Then if you were offered shoddy clothes or rotten rice, you could throw these back at those who gave them. In spite of my efforts I could not get them to see the matter in this light. Yet these people had not been dependent and helpless earlier. In their past lives they had held suitable jobs in the village and worked for their livelihoods. They would never have descended to the level of begging. It was the life in the camps that had converted them into a class dependent on others and robbed them of their self-respect, too. What a tragedy.

Among the mass of refugees, I also saw some peasant families who had not forgotten how to support themselves. Whenever they found a bit of vacant space in front of the camp, they planted gourds, beans, chillies and aubergines and earned some money. For people who were used to living by the sweat of their brows, just waiting for handouts was a tragedy too deep for words. A number of peasant families were sent to Dandakaranya and various other places, where they were given plots of land to cultivate so that they could resume their lives as farmers. Much of this land was barren and rocky but they poured their life-blood into it, made it fertile, and succeeded in growing crops. I did not have the opportunity of seeing this for myself, but I heard about it and saw the newspaper reports. The skirmish at Marichjhapi is proof enough of the fact that all refugees have not been able to reach such a state of resettlement even now.

When those who were not peasants also realized that there was no point sitting at home, then they too began earning their living. I noticed a positive awakening particularly amongst women. Had they not been uprooted this change might not have occurred so quickly. I was often on tour, and whenever I boarded a train I would run into these women who travelled up and down, crowding the compartments meant for women, and for men too. When I got talking to them, I learnt that some were at school, some at college, while others were teaching. I would very often get to meet women from Barishal. Indeed, I had not known that there were so many people from Barishal! I toured almost the whole of India, and everywhere I heard the unmistakable accents of Barishal. I used to feel good thinking that people had once ridiculed us so much because there were no railways in our district, and today we were boarding trains and ploughing through vast areas to reach any destination in perfect ease. And what about the women? Even young girls were getting on and off stations, all by themselves. They were not afraid to travel all alone in search of a livlihood. Had they stayed within the district, they might not have acquired this self-confidence. It was not just their lives; these women were able to take the responsibility for maintaining their entire families. They were no longer a people who were drifting, lost and overwhelmed. They had merged into the huge ocean of humanity in West Bengal. These women from East Bengal were teachers or nurses or clerks; was there any work that they could not do? They formed the majority of the working women of West Bengal. This is just one example of how women who had once lost everything helped the women of West Bengal to enter the job market, something that has probably not been realized by anyone. Had it not been for the pressures of necessity and numbers, it might not have been possible to push open the doors that had remained closed to women all these years.

These people became a source of strength to the Party, though our own responsibilities also increased. There was no limit to the numbers of colonies that were set up in the eastern, northern and southern outskirts of Calcutta. We were present in almost every place. After overcoming police repression we set up units of our samiti in almost every colony. We were on the move all the time. I began to find new friends in the colonies every day. Apart from my acquaintances from East Bengal, I got to know many other women who were active in our samitis. Many new samitis and working centres sprang up in these colonies, and women such as Renu Ganguly, Kabita, Kamala and Basanti came forward as organizers. Gradually all of them matured and developed into seasoned activists. Later they also became party workers. Every colony seemed to be a base for struggle, and I did not feel like leaving whenever I visited them. It seemed as if I was in Barishal itself; I would get to meet those simple, unaffected and intelligent people.

None of these new samitis affiliated themselves to the Mahila Atma Raksha Samiti; they wanted to maintain their independence. The colonies had taken the names of national leaders, and so we had a Nehru Colony, a Gandhi Colony, a Netaji Nagar, an Azadgarh, and so on. In spite of the people having been beaten up a hundred times they had not changed the names, and the mahila samitis took on the names of their parent colonies . Women and men, all were aware of the need to organize, and no obstacles were put up by the families to the formation of these samitis; on the contrary, there was a lot of enthusiasm. All women could become members. What appealed to me tremendously was that when there were any general meetings or conferences, these did not remain confined to women alone; men also participated in them. The number of samitis started increasing gradually. We could not meet their demands for help from our central organization. Later, when all these samitis and our Mahila Atma Raksha Samiti units coalesced into a central women's federation, our functioning became much simpler.

Either, Neither, or Both

SHEHLA SHIBLI

I t was early in 1946 that I decided to get married—to Shibli, a Muslim. By then he had contributed seven succulent *raans* (legs of sacrificial animals) to the household over seven Eid-ul-Azhas and I was impressed. My family, who had partaken of the same *raans* and enjoyed eating them, remained unimpressed to the extent of disapproval. They said the times were wrong for inter-communal marriages, which could overnight become inter-national and cause problems. Friends, they told me, had been known recently to turn into enemies in some cases. Etc., etc.

But since they saw that the taste of the *raans* lingered on my lips, Father declared all our property as refugee property, including our Model Town bungalow which he had originally put in my name. In this he listened to the advice of his next-door neighbour and friend, Sardar Nihal Singh, who told him that my life would be made unsafe by Muslim predators who would think nothing of plunging a knife in my chest to acquire the property. My father shuddered, looked into Shibli's innocent eyes, and wavered. But he was in strong hands, which held bridge cards evening after evening when four friends sat together to dissect the political situation changing around them. He succumbed, and soon after left Lahore to join my brother in Delhi, where he had set up his medical practice. He had chosen Delhi because Father had too many friends in Lahore, all entitled to free medicines as well as advice.

Why Father left is another story. With the turn of the tide, all his personal staff of servants, Muslim as well as Hindus, left. The huge bungalow remained unswept, while garbage piled inside as well as outside on the road. Lawns were littered with fallen leaves, broken twigs, and the eleven *seers* of milk which our pedigree cow delivered daily remained curdling in pots and pans, till we fell short of utensils to hold them. Our *gawala* was the only worker who continued his daily visits to milk the cow, to our extreme discomfort. After Pakistan was declared, my husband and I gave the cow to him as a present, because there was no grass left in the fields to feed her. The cow, when he pulled her ropes to draw her away from the house, refused to budge. But when at last she felt she had no recourse, kept turning and looking back at us in sorrow, and there were tears in her eyes.

Nor was the accumulating milk the only serious problem Father had to encounter. My infant son's napkins had grown into a menace with his running tummy. There was no way to fight this, as my Ayah had deserted us. Then there was an accumulating number of milk bottles facing Father, a heart patient. When my sister-in-law blamed him for his heartless partiality in choosing me against her and my brother, and remaining in Lahore for my sake, he gave way and left.

Brought up in the wilds of Kashmir in a progressive family of Hindus, we had remained totally unfamiliar with problems of race, creed, or colour. Our coterie of friends had always included boys and girls of every kind and community. Our servants were selected with the same sentiment. My very first Ayah in Jammu had been Mehro, or Mehr Bibi, and the second in Kashmir was Janan—again a Muslim.

If we found a difference in the mode of living, praying or eating of our friends and staff, neither we nor our parents felt alienated, since the same God, we were told, had created us all. He had delighted in creating a vast variety of people in the Universe and so should we delight in it. We did.

The main divisive difference that made the orthodox hostile was that Muslims were meat-eaters, including the flesh of beef. The orthodox among Hindus were vegetarians and spurned this practice of killing animals, specially resenting the killing of the cow which yielded milk. This made them exclude Muslims from their kitchens even when they befriended them. We, a family of meat-eaters, had no such problem with our friends, and shared our meals with them happily.

There were other divisive practices which were created by forces alien to our way of thinking. It seemed funny to us that while all Hindu girls in schools were taught Hindi and English, Hindu boys learnt Urdu and English. That may have been one of the reasons for my early rejection of the primitive local school, considering my deep interest in Urdu poetry and the ghazals we went about singing in the house. The immediate cause, however, was when I saw the Head Mistress open out the hair of a young lower middle-class girl, and comb it into a tight plait before the whole class. This kind of indignity, even though there was not the remotest chance of it coming my way (my father being a member of the Board of Trustees, for one thing) could not be tolerated. No amount of persuasion would make me enter the premises of the school again. A bright Kashmiri teacher was engaged to coach me at home. His name was Shri Dhar Joo Kachru and he took me right up to Matric level. My brothers' Urdu teacher was Master Hukam Singh, from whom I also took lessons.

By the end of September, the tourist season in the beautiful valley would officially be over and visitors would have left for their homes. So would the sons and daughters of officers studying in colleges in the plains. We would then find ourselves shut in the valley with only a few families, and consequently grew close to them. There were the families of Ministers in the Kashmir government to meet, and doctors, businessmen and politicians, and palace parties for our parents to attend. We made friends with their children, played and shared confidences irrespective of their religion. For there were several Ministers who were Muslim. There was Nawab Khusro Jang, Maulvi Nazir Ahmad, Abdul Qayyum, etc. There was a doctor named Abdullah, whose daughter Naima became our friend, specially after she joined Kinnaird College in Lahore. I followed her there later.

What I noticed, even as a teenager, was that while girls from Muslim families were all our friends, the boys were kept apart, and though we saw them moving about and sometimes salaaming us, they didn't join our play groups, the only exception being Ejaz, the son of Minister Qayyum, who would visit us with or without his extremely beautiful mother, Mahamuda, who was friends with my mother. Always a loner, Ejaz seemed to take his mother's early death very hard.

We lost sight of him for years, until I came across a news item in a local daily some years ago. Ejaz had committed suicide in London. We were all horrified and saddened.

Among our particular friends were Balraj Sahni, his brother Bhisham and their several cousins, and when I say several, I really mean just that, for there were hordes of them. Balraj later came to be known as a film actor and a writer, having secured awards for both. Bhisham, now a great writer in both Hindi and English, was my classmate in Government College, Lahore, later. Though Balraj is no more, the rest of us who are still up and about remain 'thick as thieves', and meet in Bombay and Delhi almost every year. In our fold now are also his nephews and nieces and their children and grandchildren.

India's Independence Movement, which had been triggered after the First World War when the British rulers made promises of bestowing partial self-rule on us in return for utilizing all kinds of our resources, in men and material, and then failed us, had gained momentum when the Jallianwala murders took place in Amritsar, in which all who attended a meeting were hacked to pieces by orders of Generals Dyer and O'Dwyer. Now, years later, the freedom movement was at its peak, with

Mahatma Gandhi's launching of his 'non-violent non-co-op-
eration' protest against foreign occupation of the subcontinent,
and the resultant high-handedness of the rulers imposed on
the country. We were directed to boycott all foreign imports,
and discard the foreign clothing which only fed their Lanca-
shire mills and impoverished India. Instead, we were asked to
promote our cottage industry, take to hand-spinning as a sym-
bol of our declaration of independence. The spinning-wheel
movement sprang up overnight, and wearing home-spun clothing was taken to by all freedom lovers, Hindu, Muslim, Christian and Parsi alike, with enthusiasm. I refer to the Raja of
Mahmudabad's statement made after the Jallianwala massacre: 'The interest of the country is paramount, whether we are
Muslim or Hindu...'

We were united against a powerful foreign enemy. The All-
India Congress was the common platform for all, and included
people like Mr. M.A. Jinnah, Maulana Azad, Hakim Ajmal Khan
and Dr. M.A. Ansari, who held the presidentship of Congress
at one time.

Though removed from the mainstream of action in the far-
away, rarefied atmosphere of the Kashmir valley, the intense
movement had managed to seep into every home, till all of us
in schools, colleges and at home were wearing khadi, cum-
bersome and heavy as it was, and feeling proud of being a
part of the great movement. Some of the boys of our acquaint-
ance even became active revolutionaries and plunged right
into the heart of the movement.

I remember one of our friends, a young boy named Prem
Dutt (not to be confused with the great revolutionary Bhagat
Singh's friend, Dutt), who joined the same group and gained
instant fame by throwing a shoe at a magistrate in a Lahore
court, where the Bhagat Singh Conspiracy Case was under trial.
He was confined to prison for years, where he turned himself
into a linguist and scholar with a long beard. He certainly made
good use of his detention.

While many of the freedom fighters returned their titles and the *jagirs* bestowed on them by the British rulers, my sole contribution to the non-violent movement was, perhaps, only sticking to khadi apparel and applauding the sacrifices of others.

Later, in 1920, tables started to be turned when the Arya Samaj leader Swami Dayanand started his *shudhi* movement with the mass conversion of some lower-class Muslims. This horrible move by one fanatic rightly angered and alienated the Muslims, until the newly-formed Muslim League broke up. Disgusted with the way things were turning, Jinnah took himself off to England and remained there till 1937. On his return, he suggested the formation of a Muslim League- Congress Coalition, but failed to settle the terms. This was the first sign of the parting of ways to come.

Those of us who were not old enough to absorb the implications of the political currents working in our midst remained untouched. Brought up in the lush valley with dancing rivulets and prancing horses, those friends with whom we shared this experience will ever remain close to our hearts. We will remember the shared deep silences of winter, the haunting melodies like *Goshe Matija na no* ringing through the hills, or hummed by a lovely paddy grinder—that vision of a celestial being—a young girl dressed in rags in a stance which would put a queen to shame.

Qudrat-Ullah Shahab was also roaming about in the same sphere, his brother being a doctor in the State Hospital. He was a friend of my brother. Lately, wading through my books, I found two, *Silas Marner* and *Scenes of Clerical Life* by George Eliot, with the inscription, 'Presented by a friend to J.C.B. as a humble token of love for his literary intellect', signed Qudrat-Ullah Shahab, dated 15 July 1936.

Our family entered the valley in 1926 when my father was posted in the Civil Hospital there on his return from Edinburgh, where he had gone for his FRCS. I remember the first evening we walked into the house allotted to us. It was on the outskirts of the hospital in Srinagar in Mira Kadal area on the banks of the River Jhelum. My elder sister opened the windows of our bedroom, and there was the River Jhelum with *shikaras* plying on it, and the *manjies* (boatmen) singing lustily. There were only a few house-boats, mostly vacant, it being the month of November when visitors had long departed for warmer climes. The trees had shed their leaves and stood in their bare majesty on the other side of the bank, while Mount Shankracharya, now known as *Takht-i-Sulaiman,* loomed in the distance, looking remote and yet approachable. We were awed, and fell under its spell. Friendships that we formed in such surroundings could not be torn from our hearts, nor the nostalgia wished away easily. It has become a part of us.

Sometimes, accompanying father on his nightly hospital rounds, I would see many Muslim women with their stomachs burnt. This kind of accident was common there, and was caused by *kangris* which the poor carried hidden under their gowns.

I asked my father how these people could be poor when the gorgeous valley they lived in was fragrant with rich saffron fields ripening under the sun, and factories around producing costly pashmina and lovely silks. How could anyone lack for food either, when the trees were dripping with ripe cherries and peaches, and there in the fields grew luscious strawberries waiting to be picked. All this was theirs, wasn't it? They were the original inhabitants of the valley, weren't they? So why...?

My father sighed, as if under great pressure. "I know what you mean. All this is theirs, and yet not theirs. You will understand when you grow up."

"But do *you* understand?" I asked, puzzled.

"Probably not, or only partially. It is painful to see so much poverty," he said, sighing again.

"I don't want to wait till I grow up to know, and that also only partially. I want to know it all now, this minute," and I burst out crying, because that day I had seen our driver, Ghulam Mohammad, son of our Ayah Janan, carry his little sister into the hospital. Her tummy had third degree burns on it. Noori was a beautiful child of seven who would sometimes come to the house with Janan and play with me. I had taken her to heart, and so had my parents.

What would I learn when I grew up? As it happened, quite a lot, and that was mostly about my own helplessness to do anything for the people of the valley I loved so single-mindedly.

Visitors to Kashmir came from all corners of the world, and included unknown figures from the world of art and literature with whom we were to grow closer and closer as we grew. Among them were people like the famous poet of the continent, Faiz Ahmad Faiz, Sufi Ghulam Mustafa Tabassum, Rashid Ahmad (later Director-General Broadcasting, Pakistan), artists like Ahmad Saeed Nagi, and S.N. Sanyal, who was later to marry a first cousin of ours. Dr. Taseer came, and worked in the valley as Principal of the Sri Partap College after we had left.

And one day a visitor announced was Swami Dayanand, about whose *shuddhi* and *sangathan* programme we had heard of with extreme distaste. A fanatic amongst Arya Samajis, he had single-handedly been responsible for creating friction between the two major communities of India, Hindu and Muslim, and to our delight my father refused to have anything to do with him. If I were to say that every Hindu we knew felt the same way as my father did, perhaps I would not be correct. But if they felt any different, we younger members of the family had no means of knowing. It didn't, however, stop us from wondering why some Arya Samaji friends considered him worth entertaining.

Among my father's associates was the rebel Sheikh Abdullah, later known as the *Sher-e-Kashmir*, who was trying to wrest the rights of Muslims from the Hindu Raja Hari Singh. I remember his wife, the daughter of Kashmir's famous hotelier, Nedou, who became a staunch Muslim. Her favourite song was:

Muskurate ja rahe ho, dil ko tarpane ke bad
Bijlian chamka rahe ho, phul barsane ke bad

There she would sit, confident of her expertise, surrounded by smiling faces while she ran her slender fingers over the keys of a harmonium. I refused to smile, because she had told my sister (with a wink) that I shouldn't be allowed to wear rouge at such a tender age. To disprove this unfair charge, I had washed and washed my face until it got redder and redder. No, I didn't smile. Instead I laughed and laughed at her accent.

We got to know many Kashmiri families. There was Bakshi Ghulam Mohammad and his brother Majid, fond of clowning; there was Ghulam Sadiq. All these people, including Sheikh Abdullah, were dealers in pashmina, silks and carpets, and owned huge factories. They would hold rallies and demonstrations against the Dogra ruler of the state and his partisan policies. As the Chief Medical Officer of the state automatically became ex-officio superintendent of jails, Father in this capacity got to know, and became very fond of, these daredevils. If they smuggled cigarettes or notes in prison, Father would turn a blind eye to them.

Once he was summoned to the palace and charged with over-friendliness with Christians and Mussalmans. The Maharaja, who was fond of him, said to him, 'I hear you have a soft corner for them, and frequently share their meals also. As such, we refuse to have you at our table, or shake hands with you. You have become one of the untouchables for us.'

Father smiled and said, 'Your Highness is right. I not only eat with them, but receive their vomit and their urine on my body when they are ill. But what worries me is that you, Your Highness, have been eating your meals with this untouchable of the lowest kind, and even embracing him. I think by now you are equally contaminated. I am afraid nothing can purify you now. Please discuss with Swami Dayanand how to get purified. He has a huge *shuddhi* programme—maybe he can make you a Hindu again.'

Luckily, the Raja saw the humour of the situation, and again enfolded him in his embrace. Since he was already contaminated, I suppose he thought one more time wouldn't matter.

In 1937 we had to leave Kashmir because of Father's health problems, and settled down in Lahore's Nisbet Road, near our grandparents. As by now we were all of us studying in Lahore and going home to Srinagar only for our summer vacations, we soon adapted ourselves to changed conditions. When our Model Town bungalow was built and ready to receive us, we shifted there in 1938.

Next year came World War II.

I was in Dalhousie convalescing after an attack of typhoid. I was also trying at the same time to work out a solution to a scrape I had got myself into through a disastrous marriage.

'We are at war,' I heard King George VI's voice announce. I looked at my counterpart in the episode of disaster and declared another war, on the personal front.

On returning to Lahore I joined All-India Radio as a reader and selector of material for broadcasting. A few months later I went through an interview to get into the regular cadre of AIR, was selected and posted to Lahore, where I shared an office with Hafiz Hoshiarpuri the poet, and Agha Bashir Ahmad, who ended his career in Pakistan as Director of Pakistan Television in Lahore.

I found a flutter of activity at the station. War was on, and though not India's war, strictly speaking, our soldiers were fighting on all fronts. Every radio programme we put forward was geared to the raging war. There were messages to be sent overseas and received, entertainment programmes to be planned and projected. No matter what programme portfolio we held, all of us had our hands into everything. Anyone could find himself (or herself) suddenly called upon to become an announcer, a newsreader, a writer, an interviewer or a producer at an instant's notice. The next moment the same person would be required to fulfil the duties of a public relations officer to important speakers or world famous personalities, scientists or historians, people like Professor Toynbee, writers like E. M. Forster, artistes like Ustad Bare Ghulam Ali Khan, or dancers like Uday Shanker or Ram Gopal—in fact, the works.

We would scour the town to hunt for talent, from drawing rooms and clubs, from village *mailas*, and from the red-light area of Lahore, Hira Mandi. We would pull out speakers from government offices, from women's associations, and children from their schools. An alert eye had to be kept out for spotting important visiting celebrities. The cars at our disposal would forever be on the roads, despite strict petrol rationing, even for buying presents and chocolates for performing children. On days of late evening transmission duty, I would take a servant along and grope my way through streets, pitch dark because of blackouts. All hours were working hours for us, as broadcasting was an essential service. The more demanding the work, the closer we all drew, irrespective of our caste, creed, social status, or communities. We were knit in the camaraderie of a common heritage. All broadcasters became ours, whether they were visiting artistes or local ones, from Gangubai Hangal, Timir Baran or Begum Akhtar to classical dancers Uday Shankar and Ram Gopal, from poets Akhtar Shirani, Josh Malihabadi, Faiz Ahmad Faiz, Miraji, and editors of newspapers and magazines. The station had recruited the most talented of the country's intelligentsia to its staff, which included writers like Krishen Chander, Mahmud Nizami, Rajinder Singh Bedi—in fact, the top talent of the country. Petty problems which divided communities never had a chance with us. The dramatists we worked in close communication with were no less than Rafi Peer and Imtiaz Ali Taj.

The families we grew close to comprised almost the whole of Lahore—the Manzur Qadirs, the Fazal-i-Hussains, Justice M.H. Rehman and his brother, Rahim. There were many Christian families, the Sondhis, the Chatterjis, the Singhas, the Bhanots, the Ram Chandras, etc., who were prominent educationists, and our friends. We had a vast coterie of Hindu and Sikh friends also. There was N. Iqbal Singh, and K.S. Duggal, writers and colleagues. N. Iqbal Singh, the writer of *Andaman Islands*, was for some reason referred to as 'Ikki, my love', and was called that till he died. Duggal, several of whose books lie on my shelves, married a girl from a top Muslim family who is a doctor. There was the volatile and prolific writer, Khushwant Singh, and his handsome wife, Kanwal, great friends of my sister and brother-in-law, Som, and bosom friend of Manzur Qadir, and his wife, my dear friend Asghari. In 1979, when I was a guest at her daughter's house in Washington, D.C. along with my son, Asghari regaled him with stories of my college days, such as when cycling with my brother on Davis Road, we were laughing so much that we both fell off our cycles.

Life on the personal level soon ceased to be a bed of roses for me, in the wake of a couple of heart-rending deaths in 1942, so I made up my mind to go away from Lahore and opted for Lucknow. I found it just the place for shedding my blues, and was utterly enchanted with its aristocratic charm and old-world hospitality.

The music that emanated from the Lucknow studio of AIR was nothing short of pure inspiration. And no wonder. The artistes at the disposal of the station were some of the topmost musicians of the era, people the subcontinent would boast of for ages to come. They were Ustad Alla-ud-din Khan of Mahiar, sarod nawaz; Ustad Sundu Khan, sarangi nawaz; Ustad Fayyaz Khan, vocalist; the young and upcoming Ustad Ali Akbar Khan, sarod nawaz, the son of the maestro Alla-ud-din, with magic in his fingers. Surely he was on his way to vie with, and perhaps outshine, his illustrious father-in-law, Ravi Shankar, the sitar maestro. There was Rasoolan Bai with her melodious thumris, Akhtar Begum the enchanting singer with her sparkling dadras and chaitis, and many others.

Many a morning I would wake up in the early hours and go to Ali Akbar's house to hear him practise in the next room, while I sipped tea with his wife, drowning myself in the music. On other mornings Akhtar Begum would breeze in, put me in her car, and take me home with her. Akhtar was married to a tall handsome barrister from a taluqdar family, Ishtiaq Hussain. "I am keeping a tiger in my den," Ishtiaq Bhai would say, referring to Akhtar's volatile artistic temperament.

At the studios, Rasoolan Bai would draw me into the music studio and sing me her latest thumri. No, I was not in charge of the music section. I was put in the Features Section, where I was in close touch with the humourist, Shaukat Thanvi. Shaukat Bhai was a dynamic writer, scribbling away while he talked, turning out four or five copies of his features, handing them to the seasoned actors in our live studio, while I sat on the control panel, manipulating the switches with trembling fingers. No rehearsal was possible. But our artistes coped, though I still shudder when I recall the nervous tension this caused.

The atmosphere at the office was friendly and relaxed, and conducive to creative activity. The window of my office looked out on to a magnificent garden area, with a huge leafy tree with over-hanging branches. During barsat, it would gather into itself the darkness of the looming clouds, and scoop up the showers in its foliage, reluctant to let them go. I would watch the whole scene with fascination, and thought of it as an embodiment of the grandeur of the spirit of Lucknow.

Our broadcasters included the top intellectuals of the day living in the UP, among whom were the great poet, Firaq who was specially partial to me. There was Niaz Fatehpuri, Sibte Hasan, and my friend, Dr. Rashid Jahan, and her learned husband, Dr. Mahmud. Dr. Rashid Jahan was the sister of Khursheed Mirza of PTV fame. We would look forward to having a bite with her often, specially when she treated us to besani roti with bhindi bhujia. My friend, Maya Sirkar, was there, living on Cowper Road. Later she married M. Jamil, came to live in Pakistan with him, and worked as Reader (and then also as Head of the English Department) at Karachi University. Attia Hossain, who was known as the number one beauty of Lucknow (and later became Attia Habibullah and worked for the BBC in London) lived in Lucknow and since her sister-in-law, Asif Rishad (the youngest daughter of Sir Fazal-i-Hussain of Lahore) was a close friend of mine, I came to know Attia well.

But alas, my days in Lucknow were numbered and approaching their end because of my servant, Bakhtiar Ali. My old family servant Ram Singh who had accompanied me from Lahore, had left, and I had substituted him with Bakhtiar Ali. A war veteran, Bakhtiar Ali had been discharged from the army because of shrapnel wounds, and had become my cook-bearer. He was asthmatic, and stingy. One day I got annoyed with him.

"I gave you a tenner a week ago. Why don't you spend it, and give me variety in my breakfast. If you don't spend money, I'll have to let you go."

"Dussehri mangoes I bought yesterday were one rupee a dhari (consisting of thirty-three mangoes). Where should I spend the money!"

"Besides," I continued cruelly, "you cough and cough and put me off my food. How long can I put up with this? You'll have to go, I'm afraid."

"Only my dead body will leave this house," he announced, and picking up the tray, left.

Bakhtiar Ali died that day, crushed under a military jeep while crossing the road to buy eggs. Carrying a Neville Chamberlain umbrella on that rainy day, he met his end, while those of us on transmission duty waited for him to bring us our elevenses.

In the servants' quarters, his wife with one son and a couple of hens did not know about the accident. Nor did we, until a news item next day reporting a stray death brought it to our notice. We verified the news, and brought his umbrella home for his forlorn wife.

With the police force of the town behind me, Akhtar Begum's barrister husband, Ishtiaq Bhai, as my counsel, and my journalist friend Jamal Kidwai as strong moral support, a campaign was launched for getting adequate monetary reparation for the bereaved wife and son of Bakhtiar Ali. Since this necessitated my running around town at all hours of the day, I had to take days off from work. The Station Director, Jugal Kishore Mehra (who later married the Muslim artiste, Anwar Begum or Paroji, and lived in Pakistan as Ahmad Salman) and I had a serious difference over this, to resolve which the Director General, Ahmad Shah Bokhari (Patras), came over to Lucknow himself. Though Jugal by this time had had second thoughts, I elected to go to Delhi with my old professor, and re-visited my beloved Lucknow only the next year (1944) to attend the wedding of my friend Maya with M. Jamil—still another intercommunal marriage. There seemed to be so many those days, the product of a common cultural integration over centuries of living together.

My friend Sadiqa (the sister of the film magnate W. Z. Ahmad who married an actress called Nina) had recently married a Hindu barrister of Allahabad named Chander Shekher Satnam (Dr. Satnam Charan Singh), another dear Sikh friend, had married Nawab Muzaffar Ali Khan's son, Mahmud Ali Khan, and was living in Lahore with his family at the time. And all this on the personal front despite the deep clouds of dissent and disintegration gathering on the horizon. Then in 1945, Jamal Kidwai married a Sikh girl from a prominent family of the UP, Shakuntla Jaspal.

Coming to think of it all now, it seems ironic that so many of the intelligentsia should have been hunting for solutions other than those the politicians were engaged in finding. We all start life asking questions. But it seems the only ones who find clear-cut answers are politcians—and computers, having been programmed that way.

The significant fact is that none of these marriages broke up, despite the various kinds of pressures they must have had to encounter during half a century of living together. Some record this, for the historian of the future to assimilate and ponder over. Nor did some others break up which took place within the next two years before the Great Divide of 1947. These were of two of my All India Radio associates, Iqbal Malik, and Batra with whom I was to share an office on my arrival in Delhi. Iqbal married a Hindu Bengali girl, Amita Roy, also a colleague and friend. Amita and I shared living accommodation allotted to us by AIR in Babar Lane, Delhi. Batra became a Muslim in order to marry Khurshid, and went over to the BBC in London where he became an OBE as Shahid Latif.

Our announcer at Lucknow station, Aley Hasan, who also migrated to London and joined the BBC, married a girl-friend, Krishna. This marriage broke up under special circumstances— an addiction in Aley being the cause. But he never recovered from the pain of the parting, he told me, when I saw him last in 1968 at the BBC Club in London.

Then there was Krishen Chander, the short-story writer who married Salma, daughter of another famous writer, Rashid Ahmad Siddiqui, and started a happy period of married life, contining to live happily with her till his death, which in other words means ever after.

In the meantime, political events were moving along a different course. On March 23, 1940 came the Pakistan Resolution, with the demand of autonomy for units of Muslim predominance. Areas like the North-West Provinces would be grouped together to constitute independent states in which these units would be autonomous and sovereign. The Cripps Mission of 1942 recognized the concept, but nothing came of it as the Cripps offer did not meet the requirements of the Muslim League.

In 1945 the World War ended, and in August 1946 the League launched a programme of Direct Action to achieve Pakistan. It met with strong resistance from its opponents in all the provinces of the country. There were bloodbaths in Calcutta, Sylhet, Noakhali and Tipperah, with forced conversion and abductions. Not all the efforts of the Muslim League and the Congress could stem the frightful image of hostility which loomed up to engulf the whole of the subcontinent. Many relationships built over the years fell prey to a new hatred and distrust, and turmoil ensued.

I was in Lahore while all this was happening, and about to give birth to my baby. It was now the summer of 1947, and the date was April 12 when I had the first intimations to get to the hospital.

The hospital where I had been registered was the Aitchison, in the vicinity of Gwalmandi, where a friend of mine, Qamar Khan, was an RMO. The whole of Lahore was under curfew, and getting to the hospital was going to be a real problem. We required passes to get through the protected curfew area from Model Town, but did not have time to do so. I thus found myself being escorted to the hospital by my husband, driving with a cigarette in his mouth and a double-barrelled gun by his side. Next to him sat his younger brother Saad Tarique (later a Major-General in the Pakistan Army) a bachelor, also with a gun and a cigarette, tense as tense could be. In the back sat the newly-married wife of our cook with me, inexperienced and hysterical. None of my escorts had any idea of what an exercise like this entailed. Thus we passed through a ghost-like Lahore, dark and sinister, smelling danger at every step. But no one stopped us, and thanking our stars we reached the hospital. My escorts then ran to summon Dr. Qamar Khan from her room. She was taking a shower, and shouted to them to find nurses to carry me to the labour room. My husband and Saad went to the labour room but found it completely deserted. The whole staff had run out to see a huge fire which was raging in the area near the hospital. They picked up a stretcher on their own and put me on it. I was put on a table with no one around except my own escorts, the cook's wife screaming, "Hai Bibi ji" and crying loudly. Then Qamar came running, with her long wet hair covering her from head to foot, and pushed the family out of the room just in time, and I sighed with relief. Within minutes the problem was over, and the swarming nurses and head doctor were all recounting to me the stories of the fire around Gwalmandi in vivid detail which I hardly heard, for a peaceful sleep was stealing over me.

By now Lahore was seething with political unrest and exploding in communal riots, mostly around the University area, hence they were termed 'the University riots'. The tension while the country waited for the announcement declaring Pakistan as an independent sovereign state was not only tangible but pulsating.

It was at this time that a wedding in my husband's family took us all to Delhi. It was early July, and my son was just over two months old. With me went a newly-employed ayah named Akhtar, who within days married a Hindu Brahmin and left me without any remorse.

After the wedding of my sister-in-law Bilqees (who acquired a new name, Saba Zahir), on July 12 the rest of the family went back to Lahore, including my husband, while I stayed back with my father and elder sister. Bilqees stayed in Delhi because her husband, Zahir Azar, was on the Partition Committee along with M. Shoaib (later of the World Bank). She told me later that they had an armed guard of 60 to protect and escort them, two months later, up to Bombay.

On August 14, Pakistan was duly declared an independent country, and the next day British rule in India formally came to an end. India was at last free from the stranglehold of a foreign yoke after a long, long struggle. It was an occasion for great joy, but it was being spoilt by widespread reports of looting and carnage from both parts of the subcontinent. Nevertheless, frantic preparations went on in New Delhi, the capital of India, to make August 15—India's day of Independence—an outstandingly festive occasion. No police were to be posted anywhere near the site of the celebrations, where an impressive rostrum was set up. Cars were parked for miles around the site, from where we had to walk to our seats. There on the rostrum stood a beaming Jawaharlal Nehru, the hero of the Independence Movement, now the new Prime Minister of the country, nodding and waving. Sitting around him were Sardar Patel and the other members of the Indian Congress hierarchy. There also sat Lord Mountbatten with his wife, the famous Lady Edwina. Everyone was smiling and seemed at ease. Speeches boomed on loudspeakers while the audience laughed and clapped, clapped and laughed, till all track of time seemed to be lost in the ensuing light-hearted banter and general friendliness. It certainly was a great day for the whole of the subcontinent to have been able to shake off the yoke which had long held the country in subjugation to a foreign power. But at the back of our minds was a painful reminder of something lacking in the assembly. A large part of the stalwarts who had fought with the Indian Congress and made sacrifices along with them for the freedom of the country, were missing. Suddenly a great cloud seemed to descend on me, till I was clutching my heart. Wildly I looked around, desperately trying to locate myself amongst all those carefree faces, and froze. Where in God's name was I? I shook myself with an effort, and stood up in panic. I felt my sister's hand pull me to her lovingly till I was drawn to her lap with my head hidden in her neck. Horses seemed to be racing inside me, strumming against my chest relentlessly. Somebody had forsaken somebody, somewhere. Who, how, and why? Politicians seemed to have all the answers. Had I any?

Soon it was time to make a move. We wandered round for the best part of an hour looking for our car, and at last stumbled upon it by chance. We drove home in complete silence, looking unseeingly at the architectural splendour abounding all around, vast verdant lawns spread everywhere, fountains, fields, monuments. On reaching home we found our compound full of people, cousins, friends and acquaintances who had arrived from different parts of the country, and some from Pakistan, among whom was my younger brother. Our family being an amalgam of both Hindu and Muslim cultures, we were to receive news from both sides, all heart-rending, stupefying, earth-shaking.

Thenceforth, every day brought us blood-curdling stories. Trainloads of Muslims making for Pakistan were butchered, their women raped and inhuman indignities heaped on them.

A prominent economist, Brij Narain, was murdered in Lahore. A prominent Muslim of India, Rafi Ahmad Kidwai, who had set up a refugee camp in New Delhi for the migrants, was butchered. Worried to distraction, we would try to book calls to Pakistan, but couldn't get through for the operators on both sides shouting, "Pakistan murdabad!" or "Jawaharlal Nehru murdabad!" Then would come a thud, cutting us off.

There was nothing for me to do except try and get to Pakistan. I was told there was a waiting list of 14,000 passengers with the airline, and chances of getting to Pakistan alive were slim. My brother-in-law, Som Nath Chib, who had opted for Pakistan but had been made to retract, somehow managed to get me a seat on September 3. All our friends and relations were appalled. They appealed to my father to stop me from going, threw their pagris and hats at my feet, but my father held them back. "She has her commitment to fulfil. Let her go."

The scene I met at the old Lahore airport at Walton Training Centre was, to say the least, grim. There was a police cordon to stop all passengers from leaving the airport. While I stood bewildered, holding my screaming infant in my arms, a young Pakistani came up to me and said, "Mrs. Shibli, I am Hadi, a pilot, and a friend of your husband. He asked me this morning to meet you and escort you home to Model Town. Please come with me."

"My husband asked you? But he doesn't know, I mean, how could he...?"

"I wouldn't know that," and saying this, he started loading my luggage in his car, put me in a seat next to him, and whisked me away.

Within minutes, I found myself deposited outside my brother-in-law Zubair's house in Model Town, along with my luggage. I turned round to thank Hadi but he seemed to have disappeared. Instead I was surrounded by my sister-in-law and her family.

"There she is! She has come. Didn't we all say she would, and wasn't he right when he said it would be today?" And I was pulled into warm embraces, fed almonds, made to drink cold milk-shake, while the baby was taken away somewhere to be kissed and cuddled.

"You must be fagged out, with your baby yet an infant. Here, lie down and I will press your legs," said my sister-in-law, Ismat, pushing me onto a comfortable bed and resolutely taking hold of my legs, disregarding all my protests.

"He is a clever manipulator, I must say. The way he talked me into giving up our six foot mali, Omar to work for him, because he said he needs someone to look after you."

"Who?" I ventured to ask, still in a daze.

"Who, indeed! Who else, except your husband?"

"But he couldn't possibly know my programme. I never..."

"Oh, he knew all right, believe me. There he is. You can see for yourself."

And sure enough, there he was, jumping over the hedge of the lawn to join us, grinning.

He took us both, the infant and me, to my father's bunga-low nearby. And as I entered, I found the house different. There was no furniture, no carpets, no curtains, only a couple of beds without any bedding material on them. "What..." I started to ask, but my husband hushed me.

"The house has been robbed through and through. But they didn't harm your younger brother. When your cousins brought along a chartered plane to take him to Delhi, they even came to bid him a warm good-bye."

I was staggered. "Who are 'they' you are talking about?"

"It is the villagers from the nearby village of Bhavra. They looted the house, taking away everything."

I was under too much shock to ask anything further and just stared at the devastated garden outside. No flowers on the bushes, no leaves on the trees. "Relax," said my partner in life.

Then I laughed through falling tears.

"Surely the trees haven't been robbed of their leaves by our Bhavra gangs?"

"No. That is the doing of the refugees who have come to Pakistan, ailing. They saunter in from the Walton Training School refugee camp looking for lemons and other fruit, and stay to ravage the trees. They come daily, and I don't have the heart to stop them."

"Of course," I said, "though why they should stay as you said, and pull off leaves from the trees is something I don't understand."

"Remember, this bungalow is Hindu property, and they have been embittered. This is their way of finding vent for it. Please keep inside the house, and don't take one step outside. I am going to throw all your saris away. You must wear nothing but shalwar suits from now on. As it is, I am having some problems with a Pakistani Major. He has lost some of his relations in India due to the bloodbath there, and keeps hounding me, asking me to hand you over to him as soon as you enter Pakistan. He must have learnt of your arrival by now, and if I know him he will be back tomorrow. I told him he would have to walk over my dead body to get to you. Don't worry unduly. I'm working on him and am soon going to make him understand our position. In the meantime, keep out of the way, for God's sake."

I looked at him mutely, and was worried on both our accounts. What had we let ourselves into, I wondered.

That same night, Sardar Nihal Singh's servant next door was found murdered, and my security in the house tightened, but there was no earthly way to stop the baby from howling or gurgling when he wanted to. The Major came and went, heard the precious sounds of a happy baby, and slowly but surely started changing towards the indulgent father. Then his visits stopped, and we breathed freely.

I started to work in the Walton refugee camp. There I discovered all the quilts and blankets which were missing from the house, and many other articles like suitcases which the

Bhavra thieves must have spared, unless they were generous donors to the camp.

A few days later, Allah Jawai, who was an area masseur, appeared in our house and offered her services. Besides which, she told me she had a message for me. It turned out to be a historic message sent to me by the Bhavra village thieves who had looted our bungalow. This is what Allah Jawai told me:

"They say we are sorry we had to rob you. As far as your Hindu property is concerned, we have vowed to leave you not a scrap. But your life we will protect with our own, have no doubt about that. It is not only because you have chosen to live here with us in Pakistan, but also because you are the daughter of a father who saved many of our lives, giving us medicines and medical advice, free. Our loyalty is at your command."

My God. What a country! What a people! My own now. Sentiments and loyalties, it seems, have a longer life than we give them credit for. With blood-bonds on both sides of the Divide, it is not easy for us to divide ourselves emotionally.

I must tell you of an old woman from Pakistan who recently travelled with me to Delhi.

"I wonder what the old city looks like now," she mused. "I am not even sure I will be able to recognize the mohalla where we used to live. They say everything is changed."

"Then this must be the first time you are visiting India since Partition?"

"Yes, it is, and my thanks are due to our neighbours, the Murari Lals, who sent me a ticket to visit Delhi."

"How have you kept in touch with them for so long?" I asked.

"The family has been visiting Pakistan frequently. During their last visit here, they asked me why I never visited India. They said they had arranged my visa and would be sending me a ticket soon. This is the result, and I am now able to visit them in Delhi. I have an old sister there whom I never expected to see, but for this gesture of my old friends and neighbours." I saw the old woman wiping her eyes.

No, it hasn't been easy for blood relations to be on different sides of the Divide, to be called upon to divide themselves emotionally. Perhaps it will, at some point, occur to the enlightened elements of both sides that this very emotion can be used to form the basis of a harmonious relationship. Until then we will have to stay positioned as we are and remain Either, Neither, or Both.

Shehla Shibli, a creative writer from a pre-Partition family of the Punjab, has been associated with the English daily *Dawn*, All India Radio, *Civil and Military Gazette* and *The Pakistan Times*. She has also written poems and essays in Hindi, Urdu and English.

This essay was first published in Common Heritage (*Karachi: Oxford University Press*), *1997*.

Two Women, One Family, Divided Nations

MEGHNA GUHATHAKURTA

The stories told here are those of my mother and grandmother. They belong to two generations, each being related to the other as mother-in-law and daughter-in-law, but whose lives have been intertwined not only by living in the same household, but by events like the Partition which has touched and shaped their destinies.

Sumati's story: pre-Partition

I was born in 1899 to the Raychaudhuri family in my natal village of Gabtali, Sonargaon (East Bengal). My father worked in the Treasury in Mymensingh (a town 100 miles north of Dhaka) and I remember vividly the single storey house near the railway line where I grew up—and, incidentally, where I spent a large part of my widowhood. The single most important event in my growing years was my education. I completed ten years of schooling, ignoring my father's resistance and social strictures, and passed my Matriculation exam in 1917 with flying colours. This was a time when the only girls who went to school without any moral qualms were Christians, or those from Brahmo Samaj families. For Hindu, and even more for Muslim girls, education was socially restricted to the lower grades. When I passed from the seventh grade to the eighth, the neighbours started gossiping. Was my father thinking of making his daughter a magistrate or what, they said. When these words reached my father he was infuriated, and he told my mother not to let me go to school. My mother was generally supportive of my education, but was afraid to defy my father so she told me to stay away from school for a few days. But the headmistress of Bidyamayee School, where I used to study, came to visit my mother one day and urged her to reconsider the decision to withdraw me from school because I was doing so well. So my mother allowed me to run to school, which was just next door to our house, when my father wasn't looking. My father reluctantly accepted the situation. I remember this as an important part of my life because my educational background has shaped much of my life-experiences and world-view.

When I was 15 or 16 marriage proposals started to come my way, and my parents finally accepted an offer from the Guhathakurtas of Banaripara, Barisal. The Guhathakurtas of Barisal have a long and illustrious history, much of which has become legendary. They belong to the *kayastha* caste. It is said that the title of Thakurta was given to them during Akbar's reign, an entitlement to collect land revenues, though no one knows whether they retained the rights to the land.

Ramkrishna Guhathakurta was 22nd in line of descent from Nayananda Guhathakurta, considered to be the first one to establish the house of the Borobari Guhathakurtas of Banaripara, a river-port and rice-trading centre in Pirojpur, Barisal. Ramkrishna had one son, Shashibhusan, with a college degree. While on a visit to his maternal grandfather's place in Shologhar, Dhaka, the zamindar of Sripur saw him and decided he wanted him as his son-in-law. It was Shashibhusan who later worked as Nazir in Dhaka, and who rebuilt the ancestral home in Banaripara as a pakka brick house which everyone later referred to as the "Nazir Dalan."

Shashibhusan had a large family of five sons and one daughter. None of them settled in Banaripara, and the family only went there for Puja vacations. Hemchandra, the eldest son, married into the rich landed gentry and settled in Dhaka, but had strong ties in Calcutta which ultimately took him there long before Partition. Bankimchandra, the second son, became a police officer who ultimately settled in Dhaka but was posted at different places around the country. The two youngest brothers, Sudhirchandra and Sukumar, served in white-collar jobs in Calcutta and Dhaka, but they too had settled in Calcutta by 1947. It was from Kumudchandra, the middle son, that the proposal came for me. He had an intermediate college degree and he wanted to marry a girl who was a matriculate. This was a rather unusual demand at a time when the percentage of Hindu girls with a higher level of schooling was still nominal. However, friends of his who knew about my family acted as go-betweens and the marriage took place. Even my dark complexion was exempted from criticism because of my educational qualifications! I completed high school in 1917.

Kumudchandra was a school-teacher who spent a large part of his life looking for jobs. Before we were married, he even went to Rangoon in search of work. Our eldest son, Jyotirmoy, was born in 1920 in the suburban town of Mymensingh, where my father worked in the Treasury. Arati, our eldest daughter, was born in 1926, our third son, Jyotsnamoy, in 1929, and Tapati, the youngest, in 1935.

We spent eight years in Assam as schoolteachers, but after returning, Kumudchandra contracted a disease of the spine and was paralysed. He died in 1935, leaving me to fend for my four children. I stayed on at my father's residence in Mymensingh, and my children grew up together with my brother's very large family of six. I also contributed to the family by working as a school-teacher in the very school where I was educated, and when that was not enough, I had to sell many of my ornaments. All my children had their schooling in Mymensingh, but because Jyotirmoy was very bright he went to Presidency College, Calcutta, for his Intermediate. But he fell ill and had to return. He got admission in Dhaka from where he received his M.A. in English Literature in 1943. He then became the primary breadwinner when he got his first job at Anandamohan College in Mymensingh in 1944. Later he shifted to Gurudayal College in Kishoreganj. Arati was in college at that time and the younger two were still at school.

In 1946, Jyotirmoy joined Jagannath College in Dhaka. It was then that the family consisting of my four children and myself came to Dhaka and settled down. We rented a house in Wari where many professional Hindus had their residences, but already they were vacating them and gravitating towards Calcutta. In early 1947, Jyotirmoy married Basanti who was already the headmistress of a girl's school in Dhaka.

Basanti's story: pre-Partition

I was born in the village of Fatullah (now a thriving suburban town), located somewhere between Dhaka and the river-port of Narayanganj. I was told that three generations ago our ancestors hailed from the village of Kathalia in Vikrampur, part of the larger Dhaka district. The village had been washed away by the raging Padma river. Our ancestors then settled in Fatullah. The Datta family in Fatullah owned a fair share of land and formed an important part of the village community. Ours was one of the few two-storeyed pakka buildings in the village. I was the fifth of six children—we were three brothers and three sisters. My elder sisters were married early, and my second brother went away to Calcutta to train as a medical doctor, so while I was growing up there was my elder brother Nirmal, who basically looked after the whole household, my younger brother, Parimal alias Kalu, and myself. Kalu and I were only a year or two apart so we spent most of our waking hours together, exploring our village, climbing trees for the delicious fruits, combing the fields for odd bits and pieces of grain and vegetable, fishing in the ponds, etc. Our schooling, too, began almost simultaneously in the one-room village school, until I was sent to a 'proper' primary school for girls in Narayanganj. It was about a half hour train journey which Kalu and I and our friends enjoyed thoroughly, as we played all sort of games in the bogies much to the annoyance of the guards and passengers. But these idyllic days soon came to an end. My thirst for learning grew as I passed from one grade to another, and my family realised my determination to continue my education even after I reached the socially accepted marriageable age for a girl. My father was on his death-bed, but he called my elder brother to him and told him to let me study for as long as I liked. My brother respected his wishes, so instead of getting married at 18 or 20 like a lot of girls in my class, I went on to study first at Eden's Girls College and then at the Bangla Department at the University of Dhaka. It was while studying at University that I met Jyotirmoy. He was one of the brightest students of English Literature. We met through common friends. We used to attend study circles at our Professor's house and his sharp wit and intelligence attracted me. We got married in 1948. By that time Jyotirmoy had found a job in Dhaka University and his family—consisting of his mother, brother and sister—had already settled down in Dhaka. I, too, had started my career as a school-teacher before my marriage. After I completed my teachers' training in 1943, I taught at my old alma mater, Morgan Girls School in Narayanganj. From 1944 I was offered the job of Headmistress at the then Gandaria Girls School, which later was known as Maniza Rahman Girls High School. I served as Headmistress here till my retirement in 1987.

Gandaria was one station stop away from our village Fatullah, towards Dhaka and away from Narayanganj. It was also one of those areas inhabited by the professional Hindu elite. Wari was the other one. But even before Partition there was a growing migration of Hindu service workers towards the metropolis of Calcutta, and many families had begun to vacate their houses. With the onset of Partition, the rate of migration accelerated. This made for serious problems for my school in the post-Partition period, because in the early years of my career my staff consisted mostly of Hindu teachers, and many of the students came from aristocratic Hindu families in the area.

After Jyotirmoy completed his post-graduate studies, he briefly joined the Gurudayal College in Kishoreganj, and then transferred to Anondo Mohan College in Mymensingh, where his family lived. In 1946 he joined Jagannath College as Lecturer in English. His mother, two sisters and brother lived in a rented house in Wari. It was at this time that my marriage to Jyotirmoy took place and I became part on their family.

Sumati's story: Partition

Soon after Jyotirmoy got a job at Jagannath College we settled down in Dhaka, and the reality of Partition descended on us. There were no major riots in Dhaka, just a feeling that Hindus should be leaving for India because the land no longer belonged to them. So many had departed on a temporary basis, leaving their houses intact. In Dhaka, it was only after the riots of 1950 that Hindus started to flee in large numbers across the border. But the question of whether to leave or not was something that was debated time and again in each family and did not disappear with time.

In our family, too, the issue of possible migration came up. Jyotsnamoy, my youngest son, and I were for leaving. My eldest daughter Arati's wedding was being planned so she would be leaving for her new home anyway, while Tapati, my younger daughter, was too young to have a say in this. Still, it was mainly Tapati's safety and security that were uppermost in our minds. Jyotirmoy and Basanti had other ideas—they were both teachers and both had many well-wishers among their students and colleagues who urged them to stay. Jyotirmoy also had strong political convictions and was a follower of M.N. Roy's radical humanism, which meant he did not believe in Partition. But soon after, in 1949, when Jyotirmoy became Lecturer in the English Department at Dhaka University and Arati's marriage was being arranged for February 1950, everything suddenly changed.

Hindu-Muslim riots started late in January 1950. Quite suddenly, rumours of Hindus being killed were heard in Dhaka. Arati was teaching at Basanti's school and was already on her way home when news about the rioting broke. Jyotirmoy was stopped just in time from going out and Basanti too, was delayed. Only Arati was out on the streets. Jyotsnamoy tried to catch up with her on a bicycle but didn't succeed. Arati didn't reach her destination. We were worried sick and only later learnt from her what had happened.

She heard about the riots on her way home and got down at a friend's house. But this friend's house was attacked by an unruly mob and they barely managed to escape by the back door. They took shelter in the neighbouring house, from where they could hear the mob debating whether they should charge in and kill everyone or not.

Suddenly someone called off the mob, and later many people took refuge in a Hindu police inspector's house which had virtually become a refugee centre. Since there was no safe way of communicating at that point, Arati and the others spent the whole day and night in terror, their whereabouts completely unknown to us and the other families. It was not until the next afternoon that Arati was found and brought back home.

My younger son Jyotsnamoy later told us how Arati was rescued. After spending a sleepless night, the next morning Jyotirmoy's friend and neighbour, Abdul Gani Hazari who worked at the *Pakistan Observer*, was asked to help us search for Arati. It fell upon Jyotsnamoy to accompany him because Jyotirmoy was too well known. Once Arati was found she and Jyotsnamoy were brought to the office. At that time the editor of the *Pakistan Observer*, Hamidul Huq Chowdhury, called a 'riot-maker' himself, offered to drive Arati and Jyotsnamoy home in his car. Jyotsnamoy was scared. Hazari assured him that he would follow the car in his jeep without being seen. Chowdhury dropped them one block away from their home and asked them to walk the rest of the way. Jyotsnamoy thought this was not safe and said that they wanted to be dropped at their doorstep; this way his elder brother would be able to thank Chowdhury personally. Chowdhury complied, with the words " You are very scared!" After Arati's wedding the *Pakistan Observer* carried a news feature titled, "Dhaka Normal: Hindu Marriage Takes Place!!" (29 February). Arati's wedding had taken place as planned in curfew-bound Dhaka. Only our close relatives attended, and some Quaker friends of Jyotirmoy who were social workers. One American Quaker even volunteered to drive the truck which was to bring in the wedding guests because it was difficult to get a Hindu driver. A Muslim driver couldn't be trusted. Students and friends formed brigades and guarded the houses, keeping watch on the roofs at night.

This incident had a radical effect on the family. After the wedding, a big meeting took place in our house, this time more heated than the one in 1947, about whether to leave or not. The division was the same—Jyotirmoy and Basanti wanted to remain, but this time I insisted that I should take Tapati and Jyotsnamoy to Calcutta, while Arati left for Bihar with her husband who was practicing medicine there. Jyotsnamoy tried his best to pursue Jyotirmoy and Basanti to leave as well, but to no avail. Basanti said "You take your brother if you want, I have my own brother whom I cannot leave." So my son and daughter and I left together around the last week of March. Arati and her husband followed separately. Arati would go to her new home in Giridi, Bihar, with her husband, Tapati and Jyotsnamoy would accompany me to Calcutta. The decision to migrate was therefore made almost overnight!

Basanti's story: Partition

When Partition loomed before us, both Jyotirmoy and I decided that we would not leave. Jyotirmoy had been a member
of M. N. Roy's Radical Democratic Party since his early years as
a young lecturer at Anandamohan College in Mymensingh. Roy
subsequently disbanded the party, and his philosophy of Radical Humanism was kept alive through various seminars and
workshops and study circles. Jyotirmoy retained close contact
with Roy and his disciples in India who advised him not to
flee. They believed that if educated people like them fled, then
they would merely be adding to the panic. As teachers they
were both needed in the formation of a new state. Long after
the death of Jyotirmoy at the hands of the Pakistani occupation army on the night of March 25, 1971, his humanist friend
and political colleague, K.K.Sinha wrote in his memoirs:

> ... he (Jyotirmoy) always ended by saying that the intellec-
> tual horizon of young Bengali Muslims in East Pakistan was
> undergoing a revolution due to the impact of American edu-
> cational drive and scholarships. A new generation was ris-
> ing, and it was this that sustained his confidence and faith.
> This new intellectual elite was much more virile, much more
> creative and much more open-minded and flexible and he
> felt that he was sharing the joy of this new rising sun.

But we could not share this sentiment with our immediate family. The incident of Arati being stranded overnight in someone
else's house and being attacked by rioting mobs, was too spine-
chilling for my mother-in-law and for Jyotsnamoy and Tapati.
They were especially worried about the safety and security of
Tapati who was still unmarried. They wanted to leave immediately for Calcutta. Jyotirmoy and I didn't try to stop them; we
knew that for Jyotirmoy, being the sole breadwinner, maintaining a family across the border would be a huge financial
drain on our meagre white-collar salaries.

Just after Partition, Jyotsnamoy had been attending college, but while there he left for Calcutta to work as an apprentice with his youngest uncle, Sukumar, who worked as a contractor and had a sanitary engineering and plumbing firm. Jyotsnamoy was very taken with the attractions of the big city, and made many friends in the music and entertainment world. His uncle did not take kindly to this, and objected so much that Jyotsnamoy left his house and started living with a friend. He was practically jobless. Jyotsnamoy happened to be in Dhaka during the Partition because he was visiting a friend, and he remembers discussions taking place in every home about whether to move or not. It was the number one issue being discussed. But 1947 didn't make much of a difference in the lifestyle of migrating or about-to-migrate Hindu families because the borders were still open. Even in Banaripara, Jyotsnamoy found the older generation bent on staying back— they said they had nothing to fear and they couldn't believe that the Muslims would attack them.

By 1949, however, things were becoming quite tense, especially in towns where stray incidents of violence were taking place. It was at this time (1949) that Jyotsnamoy received an offer to escort an old person to his ancestral home in Banaripara, Barisal. He took this opportunity to visit Dhaka. On the way back to Dhaka by steamer, he made friends with a Muslim boy with whom he shared a passion for modern Bengali songs. As they neared the steamer ghat in Dhaka at nightfall, Jyotsnamoy began to feel apprehensive. The young boy started asking him how he would get home. Jyotsnamoy realised he was wearing a dhoti and he refused the boy's offer to accompany him home because he lived in a Muslim dominated neighbourhood. Instead, Jyotsnamoy chose to return alone to Jyotirmoy's house in Wari relying on a Muslim rickshaw-walla who promised to deliver him safely to his house. When I opened the door to him, it was the first time I set eyes on my *dewar* (brother-in-law) because he was away in Calcutta when our wedding took place.

For Jyotsnamoy this visit was decisive. Since he was not employed any more in Calcutta, Jyotirmoy thought he would be better off making himself useful in Dhaka. He urged him and Arati to take up shorthand and typing classes, and even managed to get him a job as PA to the Principal of Jagannath College where he was teaching. All was going well until the 1950 riots descended on us.

Sumati's story: migration and its aftermath

I left Dhaka with my youngest son and daughter around the last week of March 1950. We took the flight from Dhaka. I just remember that my son noticed the Baluch Regiment guarding Dhaka airport. My eldest daughter and her husband followed separately. As soon as we arrived in Calcutta, we were handed a slip called a 'refugee slip' or a 'border slip.'

Life for us in Calcutta was very uncertain. Tapati lived for a while in Giridi with her elder sister but soon I, with my younger son and daughter, were looking for a place to stay. We moved from one relative's house to another; it was always the same message: it was too much of a burden to feed so many mouths for so long; we should move elsewhere. It was difficult to find a room to rent—we could only get them through Basanti's relatives and contacts. Sometimes things got so bad that we even had to stay a night or two with the warden of a mental asylum. It was a frightening experience. My daughter Tapati remembers the sound of insane laughter all through the night. We heard that the West Bengal government was offering land to refugees but it was only a piece of land; we had to build our own house and then there was no electricity. And also, powerful people would employ *mastaans* to just take over the land. Jyotsnamoy was too young to cope with all this and not yet skilled enough to take up a full-time job, so we had to make do with whatever money Jyotirmoy sent us. In this situation, around 1953, Jyotsnamoy got married and began living separately. Tapati and I had to look for shelter elsewhere. We finally found refuge with Basanti's younger brother's family in Jadavpur, where we rented a room for ourselves.

Sabita, my daughter-in-law, was also from a 'refugee' family which was living in a house previously occupied by Muslims. When my son met her, she insisted that he complete his degree. Jyotsnamoy graduated in April 1955 from City College, and claims that his wife brought some discipline into his bohemian life. He then launched an engineering journal, and spent his life trying to give his three sons the best education so that they would not have to suffer like him. They are all established in their fields now and he feels satisfied. However, he still thinks that the family would have been better off if Jyotirmoy and Basanti had come over too, because both of them were established in their careers and had many contacts. He used to say, "I lost my father at an early age and I badly needed someone to advise me. Instead I found that I became an advisor to many—there was no one to advise and counsel me."

In 1957, my daughter Tapati married Bimal Datta of Comilla, who worked in an insurance company. She gave birth to her first daughter in 1959, and her second daughter was born almost eleven years later. She began her married life living with Bimal's brother's family but in 1967 they were asked to live separately. I was also living in a flat by then. Jyotirmoy provided for me by sending money across the border through people he knew, because formal bank transactions became more and more difficult as the days went by. My youngest daughter and son-in-law looked after me.

In 1965 the war with Pakistan was imminent. Prior to the war, during the communal riots of 1964, we were deeply worried about Jyotirmoy and his family. He had already left for England to do his Ph.D and Basanti was left alone with their daughter, Meghna. Basanti's brother's family was also affected. They escaped unhurt but were emotionally scarred. Thus, after the war, most of the family came over to India and Basanti and Meghna left for England to join Jyotirmoy in August 1964.

To our great relief, when the Indo-Pakistan war began, they were all in England. At that time many of Jyotirmoy's students urged him not to return to Pakistan but to go to India. He would always turn them down. The family, too, we would tell him again and again to come to India, but he always said no. Dhaka was where he was needed, he said. Once he was offered a post in Aligarh University but he declined immediately. After the war, Jyotirmoy received his degree and returned to Dhaka University.

But life was to prove even more cruel. In 1971, the Pakistani military cracked down in Dhaka on March 25, to quell the growing civil movement for autonomy. Teachers at Dhaka University were among the first to be sacrificed. My son Jyotirmoy was among them. They did not tell me at first. The news appeared in a Calcutta newspaper that Jyotirmoy was shot and wounded, and in another newspaper that Basanti and Meghna were dragged out and killed. My son and son-in-law hid everything from me. A few days later they told me that Jyotirmoy had been shot in the leg and was being treated in the hospital, and that Basanti and Meghna were fine. I waited for the day when they would cross the border and arrive in India. But as the war increased in intensity and my patience started to wane, my family finally told me the ugly truth: my son had been martyred, and his family was living in Dhaka with friends and well-wishers. The truth was less painful than the period of waiting which followed. Our lives had changed drastically again, just as they had on the night we waited for news about Arati during the riots of 1950. I waited for Basanti to come, knowing that our lives would never be the same again.

Basanti's story: the build-up to 1971

Life became more complicated for us after my mother-in-law left Dhaka with her younger son and daughter. It was not easy to maintain a family across borders. We had problems at home, plus we had to deal with the problems that family members were facing in Calcutta. Sometimes they were financial—Jyotirmay had to have an operation on his lungs in Dhaka, and soon after that his younger brother, Jyotsnamoy, decided to get married in Calcutta. It was an additional drain on our family resources because we had to maintain my mother-in-law and Tapati as well. I used my family and friends to help them find a place to stay.

On this side of the border political problems were brewing, which restricted our lifestyle. The Ayub regime saw increasing hostility against India, and along with it, towards Hindus in East Pakistan. They linked the growing dissatisfaction of Bengalis with the Pakistani state to the cultural and linguistic affinity that Bengalis in East Pakistan had with Bengalis across the border in India. As such, the Hindus of East Bengal came under fire as perpetrators of a culture which was inimical to nurturing a Muslim consciousness. Those who worked for a Bengali cultural identity were labelled 'Indian agents' by the Pakistani state. Jyotirmoy and I were not directly involved with any political parties, but we were part of a larger cultural movement which strove for freedom of expression. Jyotirmoy joined the English Department of Dhaka University in 1949. Both of us were founder members of the Bulbul Lalitkala Academy (Bulbul Academy of Fine Arts) which taught art, music and dance to talented young people. In a conservative Muslim family, singing, dancing, and even painting, for young men and women, especially women, were considered to be very radical. My husband, being a teacher of English literature, was very fond of theatre, but at that time very few Muslim women could be drawn into theatrical performances. Sometimes, when a play was being staged at the University, I would request some of the girls of my school to take part in it. Their parents allowed them to do so under our joint guardianship. During this period the drawing-room of our house would turn into a rehearsal room. Many talented young singers and dancers blossomed before our eyes. It was the cultural vibrancy of East Pakistan which made it very different from the rest of that country. It was both envied and feared by many Pakistani bureaucrats and state officials. When the Bulbul Academy went on its Pakistan tours, many in the western wing remarked on how middle class Bengali women could dance freely in public. But the Pakistani state became increasingly fearful of this trend, as the demand for Bengali as a state language grew apace in this vibrant atmosphere. On several occasions, with the help of my brother-in-law Jyotsnamoy in Calcutta, we even invited artistes from West Bengal to perform dance dramas like Tagore's *Shyama* for East Pakistani audiences, as part of a cultural exchange programme.

Understandably, all this was looked down upon and discouraged by the Ayub regime. As a result Jyotirmoy, like many prominent members of the Hindu community, was blacklisted by the Pakistani state for being an Indian agent. Men from the intelligence bureau were posted outside our door on a regular basis—some of whom we had known as fathers of my students! They later told us that they were even instructed to find out what we bought at the market! It was partly because of this that Jyotirmoy couldn't get a government scholarship to go abroad for higher studies. Many of his students preceded him. He even urged me to go for a one-year diploma course in Teaching English as a Foreign Language in 1959, leaving him and our daughter Meghna behind. My mother-in-law came to stay for several months to look after them, and my brother's family took turns to look after Meghna. After my return in 1960 the political situation rapidly began to get worse, and Jyotirmoy finally decided to leave for his PhD by taking a loan from the University. We hoped that with my degree I would be able to get a teaching job in England, and ultimately be able to join him there with my daughter. It wasn't until 1963 that Jyotirmoy finally left for his higher studies at King's College, London. My daughter and I then moved to my school quarters within the compound of Gandaria Girls High School.

Most of my elder brother's family was still living in our ancestral home in Fatullah where I was born and brought up. My

three older nephews and eldest niece were in Calcutta with
my other two brothers and their families. The younger three,
Shanto, Kaveri and Kanti, lived in Fatullah with their parents.
Of them, my youngest niece and nephew, Kaveri and Kanti,
were practically living with me as they were going to schools
in Gandaria, and they provided company to my only daughter, Meghna. In 1964, when communal riots hit the Dhaka
Narayanganj area, my brother's family was especially affected.
We first heard news of the riots from our local sari vendor,
Muslim, who used to sell traditional jamdani saris to our family from his father's time. He had come from the Narayanganj
area and had seen several villages ablaze. I immediately thought
that Fatullah would also be affected and sent Muslim to my
village home by train. That evening he returned with forty
Hindu women and children, all seeking shelter under my roof.
He brought bad news. The young men of the village had fled
elsewhere for shelter, with the older men in the family, including my brother, guarding the households. They had sent the
women and children to my place. Jyotirmoy was in England
and I was alone with my daughter and our maid. So before
consulting anyone, the first thing that came to my mind was to
arrange for the night's dinner and tomorrow's breakfast. I instructed Swarna, my maid, to cook a khichdi for forty people,
and to ask neighbours for help with bedding before I left the
house to consult with neighbours on what to do in this situation. Some influential community members offered to guard
the house and school compound through the night. I then
called a high official in the police force. He was the husband
of a teacher in my school, and a family friend as well. He came
over, took one look at the situation and advised me not to take
a risk by sheltering these forty women and children for an in-
definite length of time. He said the police would not be able to
guarantee the security of the women if they stayed at my place.
The best thing to do would be to move to a shelter opened by
the government—there was one nearby, in fact on the next
street. This was the ayurvedic medicinal factory of Sadhana

Oushadhalya, and it was only fifty yards from my school. Despite my reluctance to move, I went home to inform everybody to pack the bare necessities and prepare to move early next morning. The school property would be guarded by a neighbourhood patrol, with the police keeping a close watch on things.

Next morning, the police escorted forty women to the 'riot shelter', and sent a jeep for me. I told my maid to put Meghna on her lap and ride in the police jeep to Sadhana Oushadhalya. I myself decided to walk with police escorts on either side. As I walked behind the police jeep with my daughter in my maid's lap and my daughter's doll in hers, I could feel my eyes smarting with tears of anger and frustration. Was this the best I could do for the security of these people?

Sadhana Oushadhalya was a dilapidated, rambling old building, which housed a factory as well as the abandoned living quarters of the Hindu owner and his family. The minute we entered the building the overpowering stench of medicinal herbs hit us. Mixed in were the squalor and filth of a refugee camp already overflowing with all sorts of people. Our little troop of forty women and children was shown to a small room, which used to be the owner's son's bedroom at one time. It had a huge wooden four-poster bed, broken in places, with cotton spilling out of the mattress. We decided to sleep on the floor, all forty of us, in this single room. A small space with a stove was made available to us for cooking, and our neighbours promised to do the marketing for us each day and deliver it to the camp. Latrines had to be shared with others and we could barely use them. Most of us went without baths. We spent seven days like this and then we heard that the situation had improved somewhat. On the seventh day I sent my daughter and niece back to my school quarters with some friends, to have a bath, and the next day curfew was lifted and we went home. Women and children left for the villages. We heaved a sigh of relief, but already another mass exodus of Hindus was under way. Jyotirmoy had been anxious about us all through this period and I now started to seriously apply for a work permit to teach in England. In the meantime, another incident took place which was to greatly affect my brother's family.

My youngest nephew, Kanti, was in his fnal year at Gandaria boys school. He had many friends in his class who were also part of a powerful neighbourhood gang. One day they invited him to eat sweets at a local sweet shop, and then threatened him physically. After this we decided it would be best if my youngest niece and nephew went to Calcutta to join their elder brothers and live with their uncle there. They left for Calcutta in April, and Meghna and I left for England in August that year.

During the 1965 Indo-Pakistan war we were in England, but my brother was put under house arrest on the charge that he was shining lanterns to guide Indian planes during a black-out!! It must be remembered that the actual war was being fought on the western front, not a single bomb was dropped in this region. After this incident my brother also began thinking of selling off his property and leaving for India. By 1969 they had all left.

We decided to return to East Pakistan because Jyotirmoy had taken a loan from the University and felt he had to pay it back from his salary. We didn't have a penny in savings back in Dhaka, and I was eager to return to my school. We came back to Dhaka in January 1967, but had barely settled down when Jyotirmoy, who had given his passport for renewal, was informed that on instructions from the central government, no new passport was to be issued to him. This made him really angry—he wanted to go to India to see his mother and now he couldn't. He said if the government found he had done anything wrong they could put him in jail, but to deny him a passport was to deny him basic citizenship rights. Many of his students who were in the civil services tried to retrieve his passport for him but to no avail.

After the Indo-Pakistan war of 1965, air travel between Dhaka and Calcutta had been discontinued. Since Jyotirmoy could not go, it fell upon my daughter and myself to make a journey across the Benapole border once a year to keep in touch with the family. It was an arduous journey, involving air travel from Dhaka to Jessore and then a taxi or auto-rickshaw up to the border; then crossing the border, taking a cycle rickshaw again, then a train and then a taxi. This took almost 12 hours. Custom formalities too were harsh and forbidding, but we undertook the journey in order to keep in touch with the family because none of our relatives across the border felt it was safe to return to Pakistan. Once I brought my mother-in-law with us to see her son. She went through with the painful journey because it was the only way she could see Jyotirmoy. It was only after the events of 1971 that I realized this was the last time she would see him.

In 1970 Jyotirmoy was made provost of Jagannath Hall at Dhaka University. It was a residential hall for non-Muslim students. Jyotirmoy was reluctant to take up this administrative position, but his old school friend, who was then Vice-Chancellor of the University, persuaded him to do so because it was being vacated by the renowned professor of philosophy, G.C. Dev. So in early 1970 we shifted from Gandaria to the campus. Our locality was just opposite the Central Shahid Minar (a memorial to the language martyrs of 1952) With the growing tide of nationalist fervour against the military dictorship of the Yahya regime it became a hotbed of political protest, and the prime target of the Pakistan military crackdown on the fateful night March 25. My husband was one of the first people to be sacrificed at the altar of independence. Three soldiers came through the back door, asked for him and took him away. We thought they had arrested him. Later they asked him his name and religion at gunpoint, then gave the order to shoot. They dumped him outside our house. He remained conscious for four days after, but was paralysed waist down. We could take him to the hospital only after one whole day and two nights, after the army stopped shooting and attacking student dormitories on campus, and lifted the curfew. Jyotirmoy succumbed to his injuries on March 30, 1971.

We couldn't even recover his dead body, as the hospital was surrounded by the Pakistan military keeping an eye on those wounded by bullets. My daughter and I were taken into the custody of our friends and well-wishers, and then began a strange interlude of nine months. The whole country was plunged into a war of liberation, and throughout those nine months we took shelter under different roofs, often under different names, for our identity as Hindus and as families of the 'executed' was enough to put us and our friends in danger. On various occasions I was offered safe passage to India because thousands were fleeing the border. But I resisted. I felt I had to establish the cause of Jyotirmoy's death. When I went to collect his death certificate, the hospital authorities stated the cause of death as pneumonia, yet I clearly remember that it was originally put down as death by bullet wounds. This was the first indication that our history was being systematically erased. I felt that if we left, the truth would never come out. I was also in too much of a shock to be able to face my in-laws and relatives across the border. How could I give my mother-in-law the news of her son! It is true that they had been imploring us to go to India for a long time and that Jyotirmoy had always refused. Likewise myself. Many of my in-laws felt that if I had insisted, Jyotirmoy would have given in ultimately. But if I had done that it would have meant ceasing to believe in the values and ideals we shared as teachers and imparted to our students. How could I explain all this to my relatives!

Sumati's story: the return

When Basanti and Meghna came to Calcutta on one of the first flights from Dhaka, now the capital of an independent country, Bangladesh, the whole family went to receive them. It was an emotional get-together. There were times during those nine months that we thought we would never see them again. Both Basanti and Meghna were shaken but strong from the experience. We could only listen with horror as they related the stories of their trials and tribulations during the nine-month war. The crucial question now was their future. Basanti, as staunch as ever, told us that Bangladesh was the only place that she could think of staying in. Her whole career was in Dhaka, and that was where she could provide for Meghna. She would raise her, then in her teens, till she was independent and could decide where she wanted to live. Our arguments were of no use. Meghna, too, stood by her mother and refused to be separated from her. It was then that the family decided that I should return with Basanti and Meghna to Bangladesh. By now legal migration between the two countries was not allowed, except in case of marriage. But I was old and would be living as Basanti's dependent, so perhaps it wouldn't be such a problem. I left Calcutta after twenty years to return to a homeland which I had learnt to regard as strange and foreign. After I reached Dhaka, I discarded my Indian passport and applied for a Bangladeshi one as the mother of my martyred son.

Basanti and Meghna had vacated their campus flat and returned to the Gandaria School quarters. I tried to adjust to this new life as best I could. Basanti provided all the comforts of life for me. The teachers at her school would come after school and chat with me for hours. I was their common "mashima" (aunt), and some of them became good friends. I would sit on the porch in the morning and chat with the little girls who attended the morning primary school. They told me about their homes, what they ate for breakfast, their families, what they studied, what games they played. My days were spent fairly peacefully, except for the ache in my heart which was a constant reminder of the absence I felt: the absence of my son, the absence of the life I had grown used to in Calcutta, my family growing around me. Having Meghna and her friends to talk to did make a difference, but they were at school most of the time. At such times I found great solace in chatting to a retired schoolmaster from Basanti's school, Purna Babu, who was the same age as me. We would both reminisce with great enthusiasm, and sometimes he would read the *Mahabharata* or

Ramayana and I would listen avidly. But most of all I began
to read the daily papers and became interested in the everyday politics of Bangladesh. This was something amazing for
many of Basanti's colleagues and Meghna's friends. They would
ask why I was so interested in current news when their own
grandmothers were only interested in religion or family matters. I didn't know how to answer them. It was just the way I
was, I guess.

But while life in Bangladesh moved to its own rhythm, storm
clouds gathered over our family. In 1980 a great blow was dealt
to my younger daughter's family. Her husband died of a heart
attack, leaving her alone with two young daughters: the eldest
in her early twenties, about to graduate, the youngest only
nine. For three years there had been virtually no income in the
family, they had lived off their savings. I felt utterly helpless
and useless on this side of the border. Apart from visiting her
every year there was hardly anything I could do to help. Basanti
would make frequent visits and take something for the girls.
Then after three years, the eldest daughter got a job in her
father's office and things improved a little.

Even after all these years, I feel we continued to carry the
burden of Partition. Sometimes I feel I will carry it with me all
the way to my funeral pyre.

Postscript

My grandmother, Sumati Guhathakurta, died in January 1985
in Dhaka, at the age of 82, after having spent her life alterna-
tively in Dhaka and Calcutta. My mother, Basanti Guhathakurta,
died in September 1993 at the age of 73 in Calcutta, where she
had gone for medical treatment for cirrhosis of the liver, after
having dedicated her whole life to her school, students and
family in that part of the world which came to be known vari-
ously as East Bengal, East Pakistan and Bangladesh. The Partition of 1947 had played havoc with their lives and the lives of
people around them. Yet, like the lives of many great women

who can be found anywhere in this world, their lives, too, bore the mark of the strength, wisdom, generosity and gentleness of women who struggled against time and tide to make meaning out of their existence, not only for themselves and their families, but for generations to come.

Meghna Guhathakurta, a well-known human rights and gender activist in Bangladesh, is currently working as Professor in the Department of International Relations, University of Dhaka. She is also Research Associate at the Centre for Social Studies (CSS), Dhaka University and Associate Editor of the Centre's *Journal of Social Studies.* She is the author of *Amar Bangladesh*, a collection of essays in politics and social science in Bengali, and has edited *Comparative Feminist Perspectives.*

Border Crossings:
Travelling Without a Destination

RITU MENON

I t was only the other day, 55 years after my mother's family left Pakistan, that I learnt about how they travelled to India in the aftermath of Partition. You could say that theirs was among the first of the post-colonial journeys undertaken by millions of Indians, journeys that were mostly involuntary, unwelcome, hazardous and protracted; embarked upon with fear and trembling, often without a known destination and, in some cases, an unfinished journey even today, a half century later

My grandmother lived in an old house in a busy middle-class neighbourhood in Lahore, with her three brothers-in-law and their wives. In August 1947, she was alone in the compound with her younger son and several servants, the rest of the family having gone to the hills for the summer. When word of the division of the country reached Lahore, she was told by my uncle, her elder son, that she should prepare to leave because they feared violence. She refused, as did many other Hindus. Lahore, after all, was a Hindu-majority city, and it would surely be assigned to India. After the rioting in the city when it became clear that it may not, she locked up her house, tucked her keys into her waist and walked out with just a few clothes, a hamper full of essential condiments and home remedies,

some money and some gold. Left behind were the year's supplies of wheat and rice, sugar, oil, a household full of goods—
including the beginnings of a trousseau for her unmarried son.
She figured she'd soon be back.

She never returned. From Lahore she went to Dehradun, in
the Himalayan foothills, halted there for a short while with her
daughter-in-law's family, then picked up again and moved to
Delhi. For the rest of her life she moved from one city to another, wherever her two sons happened to be, a nomad without a home of her own.

When my uncle went back to Lahore a couple of months
after she had left to try and retrieve what he could from the
house, he was handed over a few bits and pieces of lace lying
abandoned in one corner of a cupboard.

Years later, his wife (my aunt) recalled the mood of that
time.

"Gyan had told me never to sit with my back to the drive—
we had a very long drive in our house in Mayo Gardens—
always to sit on the verandah facing the gate. One day I was
sitting like this and what do I see? There's an old woman, in
tatters, walking up the drive. Head covered, but her dupatta
was just like a lot of string pulled together—and I was at a loss.
Was she a beggar? A fakirni? Who was she? Anyway, I thought,
she's so old she can do me no harm, but Gyan had given me
so many warnings that I thought up all kinds of things: what if
she has a knife? Silly, really.

"By this time she had come up almost to where I was and it
was then that I realised with a shock, that it was my grandmother!

"She had been in Lyallpur, where her lands were, and had
been kept in hiding by her Muslim neighbours—the rest of
our family was in Dehradun, you see—for many days, and
then somehow, another Hindu family in the area managed to
charter a plane and they smuggled her out of the house—I
don't know how—and she arrived in Lahore.

"I couldn't believe my eyes when I saw her! And she clung to me and wept and wept... But of course, she wouldn't eat anything because she was in her daughter's house! We finally managed to put her on a train to Dehradun—it was still safe enough to do that in Lahore, it must have been around May or June of '47...

"We left on the first of August, Bhabhiji, Satto, Anand and myself, Gyan came about 15 days later on the last Frontier Mail to leave Lahore—I remember I helped Bhabhiji to pack, she didn't want to leave at all and she was sure we would all return. So was I, I never thought this was my last goodbye to Lahore—so we took down the curtains, packed everything in those huge steel trunks and locked them. The police sealed them, we heard later. But we left Mishar (the Brahmin cook) behind—he was evacuated later. Gyan and I brought most of our things with us, because we had a whole wagon from the railways, even though as I said, I always thought we'd go back. But Gyan must have known...

"It was only six or eight months later that Bhabhiji realised we wouldn't return, and asked for her things to be recovered. We had heard from the family who were living in the house on Nisbet Road to say everything was in safe-keeping, it's all with us, come and take it any time.

"So Gyan hired these trucks and went to Lahore, but went first to our friends, the Ghanis, with whom he had stayed after we all came to Delhi, and he asked Naaz whether she would go with him to Nisbet Road. She said, of course, I'll come.

"But when they got to the house, the men spread out their arms and barred their way, saying, 'You can't go in, our women are in purdah.' So Naaz said, but I can go, can't I, and they couldn't refuse. But they wouldn't return a thing—they said it's all ours. Gyan tried very hard to say, look we left a house full of things, cupboards, trunks—you know, Bhabhiji had got a cupboard full of Chinese laces which she had collected over the years, you know how women collect things—and they said, there are your trunks with the seals intact, but do you know, the bottoms had been removed and they were empty! All Gyan could bring back was a few broken commodes and some curtain rods! Of course Bhabhiji was furious—she said, why did you bother to bring these? You should have donated them to them, as well!"

My grandmother was relatively lucky. Her brother-in-law, when he tried to leave Lahore in September, was forced out of his house at gunpoint and had to take refuge with his niece—who herself was barricaded in her home by her husband, a Muslim, because her life was at risk. Somehow, with great difficulty, my grand-uncle managed to leave on a truck travelling with armed escort. But he said they would stop every few miles, point a gun at him, and say, "Should we kill you? Leave you? Kill you?" They went on like this the whole way... when he reached Amritsar (in India) he was a wreck.

You might think that those who were already in India would be spared the risk of border crossings—but if you happened to be like my aunt who was trying frantically to get to Lahore and her family from Delhi, the experience was equally traumatic. She said, "I didn't know how to get back... There was such heavy booking on trains and planes, and my husband kept sending me messages through Hindus who were coming from Lahore, asking me to return, to come home. I was in such conflict. I wanted to go, and yet not to go. Then, you'll be astonished, there were 14,000 people waiting to get onto flights to Pakistan, Muslims who were leaving India, and yet I got a booking, my father managed to get me on somehow, he was so insistent that I go back to my husband. He came with me to the airport. There—you won't believe me—many Sikhs who knew us, removed their turbans and placed them at my feet, saying don't go, they are killing all the Hindus there... These were people my father knew, they made me swear I wouldn't go... at the airport. Are you mad, they said, that you're going... Now I hadn't really thought of it like that, that I was a Hindu or a Sikh, I just thought I am a wife returning to her husband..."

About 10 million people "travelled" across new borders in India in 1947-48, in the east and west of the country, and for each one of them it was a journey that changed them forever. Many never recovered from it.

Travel as life's great voyage of discovery in the sense of the odyssey; travel as inward journey into the self, in the Forsterian mode; travel as adventure, as enquiry, as expedition, as the necessary prerequisite of conquest; travel to record and document as the great travellers of yore did—Fa Hien, Huen Tsang, Marco Polo—travel to distant places to "civilise" or bring succour, travelling companions, and women travellers accompanying husbands or fathers to the colonies…

These we know. And we know them because we have the diaries, journals, letters, memoirs, books, periodicals, first- second- and third-hand accounts that have survived in one form or another over the centuries. But the women whose journeys I'm going to speak about now are by and large lost to history, and to memory, for they neither wrote nor recorded nor recalled their experience in a form that would endure, that could be retrieved. Indeed, they would rather not have travelled at all.

This is a story about intersecting journeys, ours and theirs, as we travelled from city to city, crossing borders once again, in search of those women who travelled without a destination in 1947; knowing neither route nor map, travelling by foot or caravan, road or rail, ship or aeroplane, bullock-cart or truck. Above all, knowing neither where their journey would end, or when.

In 1989 when I went to Karachi in Pakistan to meet my aunt—whom I had never seen—my journey was utterly different. It was not my first visit to Pakistan—I had been to Lahore in 1987—but it was the first to Karachi, and my purpose could not have been clearer. Sheila Masi was the only member of our entire family who had stayed back in Pakistan because she was married to a Muslim. Always the object of some pity, somewhat concealed, she hovered at the edge of family history, a little shadowy, a bit of a riddle. Was she *okay?* What was it really like, her life, without her family around, among Muslims, in a country suddenly become "strange"—or so we thought. She had three sons, all with Muslim names—had she quite relinquished her own identity? Could she really be *happy* in Pakistan?

My questions were only slightly different. I wanted to know why she had agreed to convert to Islam, what she missed most about her past, what was most difficult in her present, what she made of Islamisation, how she related to the idea of Pakistan, to religion, to her vastly altered sense of self. I could have asked her all this on any of her regular visits to India, but I knew that for this telling, it was necessary for me to cross over, to go to her, and then with her, back in time and space, to know where her journey had ended.

She was among the first women I spoke to at length about her experience of Partition. In the course of our research we talked to dozens of others, in many cities across India and at least two, Lahore and Karachi, in Pakistan. As we travelled from place to place speaking to men and women, we carried with us not only their individual memories but, in an unexpected twist, a "memory" of undivided India. In Amritsar we felt a kind of so-near-and-yet-so-far-ness about not being able to cross over to Lahore. Or, in Lahore, not being able to visit Sheikhupura or Mianwali, so vivid now from so many memories, not our own. This was only partly a result of listening to stories about old, old friendships and old enmities and prejudices, too. It was also a kind of rekindling of personal memory which made me locate my grandparents' home on Nisbet Road in Lahore where I, alone of all my siblings, had not been born. The impatience with memory that had marked my childhood and adolescence was replaced by something so complex that it is difficult to unravel. In Lahore, forty years after Partition, I experienced such a shock of recognition that it unsettled me. These were not places I had known or streets I had walked, they were not the stuff of "my" memories. I resisted going to

Sacred Heart Convent, to Kinnaird, Anarkali, Mayo Gardens, in an attempt to dispel memory. It came flooding in.

At night, till two or three or four in the morning I would talk with friends whose families had come (gone?) to Pakistan from Rampur, Delhi, Aligarh, Hyderabad, Lucknow. As we talked we resurrected so many memories that we found ourselves interrupting each other, often anticipating what was about to be said so that the outlines became blurred again. We had to remind ourselves that we "belonged" to two different countries now.

It was this sense of being physically present in one country but emotionally connected, powerfully, to the one left behind that imbued the accounts of almost all the women we spoke to, many of whom had never ventured beyond their villages before. Except Bibi Inder Kaur, who said she never looked back.

"I suffered no irreversible loss" was how she put it, even though her journey from Karachi to Bombay was fraught with anxiety. She said,

"It was like this: we were in a queue to get onto the ship; there were no tickets for berths, all we could hope for was deck space. There were separate queues for women and men. So my husband was in the men's queue and I was in the women's line with my three daughters. One was in my arms and the other two behind me. And there were two more, my cousin's widowed sister's children. More precious than my own because she wouldn't be able to have any more. So there were three of mine and these two, five children with me. My husband was on the men's side. And the crowds, the rush, because everyone wanted to get onto the boat somehow. The coolies threw in our luggage. Now with all the pushing and jostling, my two young daughters got left behind. When I reached the deck I realized they were not with me. I thrust my youngest daughter into the arms of a Sindhi woman standing next to me and, wailing loudly, went to look for the other two. My god! What if someone had seized them and whisked them away? Pulled them to one side? I was so worried, but at last I found them right at the end of the queue. How did you get left so far behind, I asked them. We don't know, they said, there were so many people pushing us... we had these children and we were being pushed around so we thought we would wait at the end of the line. How could they know what might happen to two young girls in such a situation? I thanked god that my girls were unharmed and that my honour was intact I boarded the boat and thought, now even if the boat sinks I don't care, I'm not worried."

Bibi Inder Kaur's completely unplanned, unanticipated journey from one country to another transported her into another realm altogether. Forced to supplement the family income she was propelled into educating herself—her own schooling was only upto middle school level—and eventually into an independent life. She separated from her husband, taught at a women's college for many years, and ended her career as Principal of a college in Amritsar.

We met her there. Each time we left Delhi, we experienced that quintessential element of travel: that which cannot be predicted, no matter how well planned the journey, but nothing prepared us for Amritsar.

Every evening, at sunset, the border between India and Pakistan at Wagah—about 30 kms. from Amritsar—witnesses a most extraordinary ritual, the lowering of flags by both countries on either side of a strip of land which belongs to no one. The "border" is a diagonal white line that runs across the middle of the road. On either side the Border Security Force and the Pakistan Rangers have their posts—modest, one-storey buildings facing each other, just the minimum architectural accoutrements on them. A portrait of Jinnah on the Pakistan building, Gandhi on the Indian. Conspicuous by their incongruity are two large mirrors just outside each building, also facing each other, reflecting what's happening on either side of the "border". Indeed, the 15-minute ritual of lowering the flags at sunset has the BSF and Rangers mimicking each other's drill—co-ordinated and practiced every morning, we were told—like mirror opposites. The ceremony is a macho enactment of aggression, the posture and gestures of the men designed to communicate maximum hostility. They wheel and strut, execute high kicks, accompanied by loud foot-stamping, glaring and chest-flexing. You think they're going to march right into each other's territory because they're so charged up, but they stop short of the "border", wheel around and stomp back to their positions. The only time they step across the strip is when they lower the flags. They are ritually lowered, cross-wise, by the BSF and the Rangers from positions on the "enemy" side—Indians on Pakistan territory, Pakistani on the Indian side. It's a startling and strangely moving sight: the dying light, the tricolour and crescent moon and star being slowly lowered on strings stretched cross-wise, etched sharply against the sky. And the plaintive note of the buglers as they call the retreat: The day is done.

I turned from the spectacle with a heavy heart. Pakistani Rangers generously invited us to step across no-man's land and pick up a handful of "Pakistani soil" as a mark of friendship. "Whether here or there," quipped one of them, "it's the same earth, isn't it?"

I suppose so, but then I remembered the *ayat* inscribed on their elaborate minaret-adorned gate:

Against them make ready your strength to the utmost of your powers, including horses of war to strike terror into the the hearts of the enemies of Allah and your enemies, and others besides whom ye may not know. Whatever ye shall spend in the cause of Allah shall be repaid unto ye and ye shall not be treated unjustly.

The Indians have no such injunction but that doesn't mean they are any less vigilant.

The road to the joint check-post (JCP) is punctuated by a series of gates that regulate civilian entry to it. A corrugated asbestos wall, painted green with patches of dirty dried blood

obstructs the view towards Pakistan—what you can't see you
don't know. Earlier, at the BSF lookout point we looked across
to the Pakistani lookout posts nestling among the trees in the
near distance. An elaborate 24 hour watch is maintained by
both sides, but ever since the fencing was completed cross-
border traffic has all but stopped. No more informal border
exchanges between officials, no transfer of seeds, no attending marriages or watching hockey and cricket matches on the
other side. Whether or not the fencing has reduced border
tension, it has certainly drastically curtailed villagers' movements. Indeed, escalating tension since December 2001 has
compelled whole villages (minus their elders) to move in the
opposite direction—out of their homes towards greater safety.

It's a little unnerving to think that you're a stone's throw
away from West Punjab and Pakistan, that you could stroll
across and back if it weren't for the fact that you would be
electrocuted if you tried.

Wagah is a border crossing.

Earlier that day, we had been taken to see the bullet-marks
on the walls of the Akal Takht at the Golden Temple, relics of
Operation Bluestar in 1984. It was impossible to avoid a discussion of it. Everywhere we went, everyone we spoke to automatically assumed that's what we meant when we mentioned
1948. "Oh, you mean 1984..." they would say confidently, for-
giving us our lapses of memory. Bewildered at first, we soon
learnt to listen patiently to accounts of the desecration of the
Golden Temple by the army, before attention reluctantly turned
to the events of '48. In universities, gurudwaras, deras run by
the Seva Panthis or in the marketplace, whether we talked to
priests, militants, shopkeepers or ordinary people in their
homes, the two dates coalesced. The intervening years had
collapsed and memories ran into each other as the experience
of being under siege came to the fore.

When we stopped in Jalandar on our way back however, to
speak to women at the Gandhi Vanita Ashram about those
who had been abducted and recovered during Partition, it was

as if the clock had stopped at 1947. For the handful of women from '47-'48 who still lived in the Ashram, their first journey out of their homes in Pakistan and into India was also their last. Henceforth, they might travel out of the Ashram in search of daily wage labour in the city, but that was usually the extent of it. Of them, B. who was recovered and forcibly repatriated to India after more than eight years in Pakistan, had refused to make the journey at all. To no avail—she had to return. When we met her in a house of her own just behind the Ashram where she had spent several years, she refused to talk about what happened. "Forget it. What use is it recalling the past? Let it be—I've banished it from my mind." How she explained her life to her three children, and how she came to be in Jalandar will never be known.

But we met someone else who had also been at the Gandhi Vanita Ashram, and her journey was just as unusual. In Jugiana, a small town near Jalandar, we went to see Indira who lived in an INA (Indian National Army) household with Gen. Mohinder Singh and his Nepali batman, whom she had married. She, too, had been rescued as a child and given shelter at the Gandhi Vanita Ashram, where she stayed for ten or eleven years. She had come from Sialkot with a neighbour whom she called *bua*. They travelled in a military truck and stopped at Jammu for a while in a refugee camp. From there they went to Batala and she was finally left behind at the Gandhi Vanita Ashram. Indira told us that she had been separated from her mother and brothers near Sialkot, and never saw them again. Much later she heard that her mother had been killed in an attack, but to this day doesn't know what became of her brothers.

So how did she end up in Jugiana? It's quite a story. After the INA was disbanded in 1942 or '43, many of its officers and jawans settled down in Punjab and took to farming. Gen. Mohinder Singh was one of them, and he, together with a junior officer and his Nepali batman, began farming in Jugiana. They lived and worked together, true to the INA creed, sharing everything including home and hearth. When Gen.

Mohinder Singh heard about the women at the Gandhi Vanita Ashram needing rehabilitation, he volunteered his batman as a groom—and Indira was married to him. She wasn't at all happy when it was first suggested but agreed eventually, and has never looked back.

For all those who made their way across the border the passage to India was a one-way ticket. Years later, when we talked to them about Partition, it was the journey itself that most women remembered vividly. Durga Rani said:

"Ours was one of the first trains out of Pakistan. As soon as we reached Jalandar, my father got a job in the social welfare department. I was living with him in Head Junu. My own house was in Multan, I mean my husband's house. I was not well so my father brought me to his house. After that the fighting started—I went to him in April, the troubles began in August. I must have been 20 or 21 years old at the time.

"All the trains were supposed to have an armed escort of Gurkhas, but often the Muslims would disguise themselves as Gurkhas. They would climb onto the trains and loot everyone. We had hidden some gold in my little daughter's underwear in a pocket—that was all that we could save, the rest was taken away—my mother's, my own...

"When we reached Lahore, we were searched. Even Muslim women in disguise looted us, whenever they got a chance they took it, even though the first train was supposed to be the safest. We waited there for 45 minutes—other trains had also been stopped. Every time the train stopped, we were terrified. There was no police. It took us five or six days to reach Jalandar. On the way we could not even drink water. If we got out at the station we were afraid we might be killed. Sometimes we had roasted gram to eat, sometimes roti-dal. My in-laws went to Karnal, I remained with my parents. There were seven of us— my younger brother, parents, my three daughters and myself. My eldest daughter got cholera as soon as we reached—she was just four years old. We went straight to the camp. We had just one glass between us, but we got our rations at the camp.

The camp was at the DAV college—they closed the college. Tents were put up, they made temporary arrangements for water, but there was a cholera epidemic very soon. My daughter died of it.

"My husband went to the camp at Khanewal in September, stayed there for three months and came to Jalandar in November with his family. He knew we were there because my father had sent messages, announced it on stations—Amritsar, Atari—along the way. My husband was on the train to Karnal but he got off at Jalandar, his parents carried on to Karnal. My husband knew ten trains had reached Amritsar, ten had reached Jalandar and ten would go to Karnal. By then we had left the camp but someone informed my father that my husband was in Jalandar. We started looking for him and finally found him in a doctor's house. But he was already too ill. He had hidden in some sugarcane fields on the way. I didn't even get a chance to ask him how these three months had passed—he died as soon as we reached."

For hundreds—no, thousands—of women, to travel fearfully often meant never to arrive. Venturing out could entail being ambushed, injured, abducted, raped, killed, converted, forcibly married. Or it could mean embracing death. Many carried vials of poison around their necks to be consumed in case they were captured, several showed up long after their families had abandoned hope of ever seeing them again. Damayanti Sahgal was one of those who managed to survive after a most dramatic escape.

She was in Sir Ganga Ram Hospital (in Lahore) working with Premvati Thapar, who advised her to leave while she could. She fled to Kullu with one of her servants because her father refused to abandon his lands and factory. She saw the killing and looting in Amritsar, in Beas, but pressed on to Kullu—where Hindus were killing Muslims—lived in a dak bungalow where she couldn't pay the bill because all she had was a couple of hundred rupees. It was full of Jan Sanghis who had to drink themselves silly in order to kill. "Hindus can't kill without being drunk," she told us, "not like the Pathans whose children kill chickens with their hands."

But she couldn't leave Kullu because all the roads from Beas were blocked due to floods. She lost all contact with her family, but found refuge with an ex-student and finally made her way to Dharamsala where she knew the deputy commissioner, but because all roads were unsafe she couldn't get to Lahore or Amritsar. Eventually, she somehow found her way to Delhi via a relative in Amritsar.

That wasn't the end of Damayanti's Sahgal's travels. She returned to Pakistan again and again, travelling to remote villages and towns to recover women who had been abducted. She rode in curtained jeeps, lived in rest houses under heavy police guard, even masqueraded as a Muslim on occasion, and always carried poison and a knife on her in case she was abducted herself.

Our own travels seemed so tame by comparison, even though they were so clearly journeys of discovery for us, especially in Pakistan. Remembering with friends enabled us to approach the fact of Partition together, yet separately, to talk about our families, our countries, our histories and, slowly, our identities. Carefully, warily even, we spoke about religion and conflict, about prejudice and, remembering, found we had to consciously recall the parting of ways in order not to misunderstand it. To forget for a while, our family and national mythologies.

Through those seemingly endless conversations that resumed at odd times—walking through Anarkali; in the middle of Tariq Ali's film on Partition; late at night, almost asleep, feeling suddenly "homesick" for places we had left behind—we learnt to accept the complicated legacy of division and creation on either side of the border. There have been many breaks in the conversation since then, many silences; some things we understand better, others we mistrust more deeply. Yet, years later, it seems to me that this is one conversation that can have no closure, one memory that refuses to go away—a road that still needs to be travelled.

Darkness and Light

BEGUM ANEES KIDWAI

It was already March and the Camp was still an unresolved problem. We could not find a way to wind it up. The people did not want to fight any longer, nor did they want any more slaughter and killings. They had tried everything, and were aware of the gains and losses of peace and riots. There was a general hatred and disapproval of the Sanghis and the RSS,* and they had understood that they would achieve nothing if they continued to make mistakes at every step.

However, the local government was bent upon driving the Muslims out of Delhi province. They were constantly trying out various strategies to achieve this goal. They even had an alliance with the people of the (Muslim) League and some were colluding with self-styled "leaders".

One such person was a retired lieutenant from a village. He was a favourite with the officers and friendly with almost everybody. We held him responsible for getting many villages vacated. He obviously had great influence in his own village, besides enjoying a good reputation in the Pakistan office. He could get a pass for anyone he wished, could transfer land deeds to anyone he desired. One senior officer (Mr. Randhawa) had exchanged 40,000 bighas of land a relative had left

*Members of the Jan Sangh and the Rashtriya Swayamsewak Sangh.

behind in Pakistan against 13,000 bighas in a village on this side. The whole transaction was done through this lieutenant.

Why was he doing this? Perhaps greed had blinded him. Or perhaps he thought that the holdings of his relatives and colleagues were not safe, or maybe he considered this the best option in a future that seemed so dark? People used to say that the government of Pakistan had written to him to send the best farmers of Delhi province to Pakistan, and that it wanted to prove to the world that all Muslims had left Hindustan. But none of us could say this. What proof did we have? We could only conjecture and give an opinion on what we saw. Some of us used to think that sheer bureaucracy compelled him—there was a lot of truth in that. He had become a sympathiser and a helper to both, the governments and the people, and we were aware of the enormous support he had.

In my view, he himself was a nobody, like many others of his ilk. They were encouraged and put before us to harm us, to create obstacles in our way and to make sure that we failed. They lacked calibre. But our real fight was with the brain behind the scenes.

One day I met him at the gate of the Camp. I told him, "Look, don't come here every day to incite these people. Whenever they are ready to return, you land up with some message, promise or order. You're responsible for their devastation. You have uprooted them from their villages and now you don't even let them think."

He said, "I don't deny that I have brought them here but that is because, in my view, this is good for them and also for me. And now there is no question of returning to the village— the lands have been transferred. Where can we go when the land no longer belongs to us?"

"And who ordered this?" I asked, "I have already checked. The government knows nothing about it. Even the Prime Minister has no information."

"Everyone knows. It has been done by the local government," he replied. (In fact, the word government in this context was not correct. Only a senior officer of Delhi Province was responsible.)

I wanted to somehow get hold of all the papers and documents, to try with at least some proof in hand, but the documents could not be obtained. I had been hearing this for many days. Didn't trust other landlords, but it was confirmed today.

Having failed four times we were really angry. This was the limit! Whenever the matter reached a point where it could be resolved this man invariably appeared, either on behalf of the Pakistan office or with some new advice or a piece of good news from a sympathetic officer. In sheer anger we told the Assistant Commander and the Camp Commander that he should not be allowed to enter the Camp.

The next day I was standing outside, watching the crowd that had arrived from the city and gathered at the monument of Isa Khan. Just then the magistrate also arrived.

I asked him, "Has the government of Pakistan given permission to send the people of Delhi across? You mentioned earlier that they were not prepared to accept them."

He said, "No, there is no permission for the people of Delhi. But look here, we have got the permit for the villagers of Punjab. It says that a train should be arranged for them."

The train was to leave the next day and therefore many people had already arrived. Seeing me talking to him, many of them stood around listening to our conversation. One of them yelled, "Aren't the people of Delhi permitted to go?"

"Yes," replied the Magistrate, "And they are saying that the agreement pertained to the transfer of East and West Punjab. But now because people from every province have reached there, there is no room. After all Pakistan is a small country. How many people can it accommodate?"

The fellow from Delhi shouted back in anger, "Then why did that fool make Pakistan so small that there is no space for us?" The Magistrate came closer and said, as if he were revealing a secret, "You should remove this scoundrel lieutenant.

He has created this whole mess." The Magistrate's face was a picture of sarcasm and mockery.

I was livid. There is a limit to hypocrisy. "Tell the thief to steal and ask the king to stay awake!" I said. "I refused to encourage his entry here, but you managed to get permission for him to stay here permanently. And then you call him a scoundrel!"

He muttered sheepishly, "I did I...did... ."

"Yes, of course, you did, it is there in writing." I had to say this. He turned away and started talking to the others to hide his embarrassment.

February and March were extremely harsh for the Camp refugees. Policemen rarely dared to loot them now. It was their own brothers and friends who riffled through their empty pockets. Zafar Khan ruled the Camp. He and his brother had collected a lot of money from the people with the promise that they would get all kinds of work done for them. They had made an alliance with the Camp police in order to carry out their nefarious activities unimpeded. They would have people arrested on charges of gambling, and then imprison them on the terrace. They were released only after all their money had been pocketed.

One day when I went there I saw Zafar Khan holding court. There were flowers in two beautifully carved copper glasses on a clean table-cloth. Various kinds of ornaments were piled high on the table. Some boxes were also lying open. For a moment he was uneasy at my sudden appearance on the scene, but then he said, "Look, sister, so many people have forgotten to take their belongings while boarding the train. There are gold and silver ornaments, utensils, clothes, everything. Tell me, what should we do with them?"

Expressing my displeasure I said, "All these were kept safely in the warehouse. Why did you bring them out? What do you want with things that belong to others?"

He said, "I was just seeing what there is. You can distribute them among these people. I have already distributed them to some, you can give away the rest. What is the point in just storing them?"

I said sternly, "Zafar Khan, you have no right to distribute these things. It is possible that those who have left their belongings behind may write to us. The trains keep going back and forth, we can send their things through others. Tell me, whom have you given these things to? I'll take them back."

On asking for names I learnt that doctors from the hospital, the warehouse in-charge, ration in-charge, and many other well-off people had 'rightfully' appropriated the stuff as their own. Out of embarrassment, one or two of them returned the things when I scolded them, and a few others promised to do so as well. But I have no idea what Zafar Khan himself might have taken—how could one find out anyway? Of course, when he felt ashamed he did say, "I also want to do the same thing, but what to do? These people are so greedy. They persuaded me and took the stuff away."

I had everything put back in the boxes, locked them and told the volunteer, "Send these boxes with me, I will put them away along with the belongings of the other refugees." By chance I was using a small car that day and it could not accommodate the boxes. I was compelled to leave them behind. Zafar Khan kept postponing sending the boxes for many weeks and finally he did not part with them. God alone knows which poor man's stuff it was and how much he might have suffered as a result. Of course it was not just one person's things—so many had left their belongings and we couldn't find their names or addresses.

One day we got the news that some bullets had been fired in the Camp and that one person had been killed. I was frightened. When I reached the Camp I was told that many rural people had gathered in the grounds for a discussion and their so-called mentor, the lieutenant, was addressing them. The police surrounded them. Somebody tried to run away and accidently got hit by a bullet (as per the police report).

Zafar Khan made a statement, "On your advice I was trying to bring all of them on to the right path by explaining and cajoling, but the lieutenant called a meeting of the villagers so I asked the police to cordon them. This is not the place for a meeting. Some people didn't understand, they started running, and the firing began."

But when I inquired into the incident all this turned out to be incorrect. The fact of the matter was that a rumour was spread in the Camp that no train would go to Pakistan. It was true that with the help of the officers and the efforts of their leader, the local government had facilitated the lieutenant's trip to Karachi to obtain a permit from Pakistan for the people of Tihar and he did manage to get their approval. However, they were most upset because all the villagers did not get permission to go. They discussed this among themselves and the situation seemed to take a new turn. The people of Tihar who had close kinship ties within their clans were in despair and said, "What will we do over there when you all are not going?" The principal actors were, of course, more concerned about the land transfers.

The lieutenant was the most concerned. He had called the meeting for this reason and was telling people that they should not change their minds, they must think carefully.

Zafar Khan was not included in the negotiations. Perhaps he took it amiss, perhaps there was some other reason. He provoked the military men and alleged that the lieutenant was spreading revolt. He was making speeches against the government. This was a blatant lie, a fraud, but there was no one to repudiate the allegation. He arrived at the Camp with the army and ordered them to cordon off the crowd. The people were surrounded, got scared and started running. One man broke out of the cordon and was shot. The army had to take this strong action because the people had turned rebellious. They were badly harassed and frightened. Women sat around cursing the government. There was an incessant flow of visitors (leaders, workers, officers and reputed people, all came), during the next two days. Everyone who heard about it came, but the heirs of the man who had been killed got no help.

I found the lieutenant imprisoned on the terrace. Army soldiers stood on his left and right. He called out to me. Saluted. A man was going up to him with his food. Seeing him, the lieutenant roared, "I don't need it! I am not going to eat." People told me he had not eaten the previous night either. I was amazed that a camp worker could imprison anybody. I asked, "For what have you imprisoned him?" "For the offence of treason." He looked at me expecting to be complimented. On the contrary, I scolded him.

I understood everything now. I wanted to inform the officers about the whole episode because the situation had got out of hand. Hundreds of sufferers were in trouble because of these two scoundrels. It was a dangerous situation. All the refugees were scared, fearing that violence might erupt any time.

The very next day we got the news that the lieutenant had left for Pakistan. On the orders of a responsible local officer he managed an air ticket and left.

Zafar Khan was well aware that his days were numbered. We were soon going to expose all his misdeeds, the chargesheet was almost ready. Just then we learnt that he had disappeared.

The whole story then emerged— trains were leaving in quick succession, the Camp was to be closed down. He had gone to the station as usual to put the refugees on the train. He arranged for two volunteers to stay behind and look after his sections in the compound, in case the women needed something or got frightened. He suspected that we would not let him leave easily, so he had devised this trick. He knew that almost everyone wanted to see him in jail, at least for a few days. The poor volunteers kept guarding his sections for four hours. Morning turned to afternoon, and then to dusk. They got worried. There had been no sound from inside all day. What could have happened? They peeped inside. There wasn't a soul there! They had been guarding those empty sections throughout the day. They rushed to inform their comrades, but it was only when they began to look for him that they learnt that he had boarded the train. He had fooled everyone. Our investigation remained incomplete despite our having completed it.

Subhadra was very disappointed at this defeat. She used to say with great confidence, "He will die. You will see him die. The lieutenant will get all of them killed."

I think I have forgotten to mention that one day a Muslim member of the ministry came to the Camp and said, "I have not come here for any consultation with you. I want you to listen to a government order which says that everyone should return to their respective homes. The government will make all possible arrangements for their safety." A couple of men who looked like leaders began to argue with him on this issue. His poetic mind was not ready to tolerate any arguments. Very angry, he left saying, "Go to hell."

Two or three trains left for Pakistan one after the other. The grounds began to clear. The Camp was closed. We too, were relieved.

I have mentioned this earlier: that information about conditions in both India and Pakistan, as narrated by many of the sufferers, were so similar that at times we were compelled to think that someone else had planned the whole scheme, made two copies of it and handed one over to each side. The same programme was therefore implemented in both countries. The situation in Calcutta and Bihar was different, to some extent, from what was apparent here. Rowdyism prevailed there, too, in a different guise, but the structure and purpose of the riots in Delhi and in both parts of the Punjab were very similar. Initially there was propaganda in both places in favour of Hindu-rule and Muslim-rule. Police and local officers participated fully in this propaganda and its implementation. All this was done in the name of the government. The people were made to believe that both the Indian and the Pakistani governments wanted the lives and properties of minorities to be declared as insecure Senior officers used to announce this quite openly. The same statement was being made in the courts, even now.

Minority communities were intimidated, compelled to vacate villages and colonies, and gather at any refugee camp. Rural people living in big villages were told that it was not possible for officers to protect them so they should vacate and find refuge somewhere, or else go with them to the safety of a camp in the city. From there they could cross the border and enter the other country. Or they would be told that a train was on the platform, and they should go to the station. Friendless, helpless people caught in that hopeless situation would begin to walk or leave on horse-drawn or bullock-carts. They would carry their few savings with them, and no one prevented them from doing so. But barely a couple of furlongs along and they would be attacked. Thousands of brutes armed with sticks, clubs, rifles and knives would pounce on them.

One thing is worth remembering in this connection: that the police accompanied the procession as it set out, but would be sure to lag behind on such occasions. People would be assured repeatedly about the arrival of the station in-charge or the DCP, but then due to some other "pressing" duty they wouldn't reach on time. By then everything was over.

People's luggage would be snatched, even the clothes from their bodies would be removed. It was especially important to undress the women. The aged and children were ruthlessly massacred like goats and sheep, and those who tried to run away fell prey to the bullets of the police or the army. And then the army would arrive on galloping horses. They would save a few lives and get a good certificate from the officers. The wounded would be sent to the hospital, dead bodies would be stacked in carts and either thrown into pits or rivers or burnt with dry leaves, and young women, unmarried girls, were distributed among the attackers, police and soldiers of the army as their share of the loot. Even the officers got a share but their precious property was kept in the safe custody of some jailer, estate officer or revenue collector. The officer would enjoy his share till he was satiated. After that the custodian had the right to sell the loot and earn some money.

Such criminal practices were common in both India and Pakistan. The situation in Delhi was such that the machinery which otherwise took each step so carefully worked at full speed during the commotion. Senior officers regularly visited their provinces and assured the people that all their actions were as per the desire of the government. They did everything in their power to fuel the fire of division.

They would warn people about impending danger but, at the same time, express their own helplessness. "Brothers, we want to save your lives, but the problem is that only Hindus can stay here. What is to be done? We are helpless because now there are two different States. It would be better for you to leave the village." The people of the other side were told, "This is now a Hindu State. If they convert you can assimilate them. Mahatmaji has been speaking against untouchability for such a long time. Purify them and start eating together."

A government officer from the Najafgarh area got some rural people "purified" in front of him in Roshanpur, Deenpura, Pot Khurd and other villages. This officer was a great supporter of the Jat movement. When I spoke to the people I was told, "Many senior officers were present on that day. The Jats of forty villages got together and made us take an oath. Now if we do anything against this arrangement they will get together and kill us."

The Rashtriya Swayamsewak Sangh had organised a rally in Delhi in the month of December—this was the climax. The officers had not woken up even after so much bloodshed. Who did not know that the youth of the Sangh had created rivers of blood in Delhi province, north-east U.P., Ajmer, Punjab and other places? Not only the living, even corpses in graves were not spared their vengeance. The graveyards of Delhi, Punjab and Ajmer were weeping at their brutality. But this rally was organised in the capital under the aegis of the Congress government, and within a month Bapu became the target of a bullet.

A well-known freedom fighter (he was Subhas Chandra Bose's comrade and an officer in the Indian National Army), told me that in the month of September he had received news of a major incident of murder and killings in Shahdara. He rang up a police officer and enquired about it. He was told, "We have no information. You must have received a false report." When the gentleman made further inquiries and informed the police, "The report was correct. Please check and let me know," he was told, "Well, yes, one or two persons have died." He did not believe them so he went to Shahdara himself. He received no help from Delhi. He came across a police truck on the other side of the bridge. Seeing the truck soaked in blood, he and his comrades stopped it. The S.P. and others reached quite late. They said that the bloodstains proved that the truck was returning from the river after throwing away dead bodies. The workers were frightened. They confessed, but it was no use. There was no punishment. No action was taken.

So much had happened and yet both parties said, "The conflict was started by Pakistan. We only took revenge." And even today there are many Muslims who say, "All this is a lie. Hindus have not lost an iota. They reached India with all their money and belongings." One lady said with great confidence, "You must believe that they are in no danger there. They are moving about quite freely in Lahore, doing their business, and when they were leaving, the government strictly prohibited anybody from objecting to their carrying away whatever they wanted. They have brought everything, even furniture. A Muslim can never torture, but you see what they have done in east Punjab and the Princely States."

On the other hand many Hindu men and women told me that the Muslims had lost nothing—they were ruling here and are in control there. They faced no difficulties, none of their kin were killed. Hundreds of our people were killed on our arrival in Delhi. The Muslims had so many weapons. On Pusa Road and Sabzi Mandi they fought with canons!

When I was returning from Allahabad in April, I met a Hindu businessman from Amritsar. A few other people also questioned him, and he became very agitated. Swearing, he said, "It was the Sikhs who got us killed. We would happily have continued with our business in both States and stayed in Pakistan. We had absolutely no quarrel with anyone. If only Tara Singh hadn't raised his sword there would have been no conflict." When I asked him where the violence first began, he replied, "The Sikhs were massacred in Rawalpindi in the month of March, and yet there was peace. But prior to Lahore, it happened in Amritsar. The Muslims took out a procession of five naked girls in Lahore and in retaliation there was a procession of 25 girls in Amritsar. When I saw this I rushed to the police station in fear. The S.P. laughed loudly and said, "Get lost, mind your own business. Close your eyes if you can't bear to look'".

Well, the situation was the same on both sides. Neither believed that the other was facing great hardships, too, and the truth of the matter was that no one wanted to take the trouble of seeing, knowing or understanding the other.

Begum Anees Kidwai (1902-80), a social worker, came from a family of staunch nationalist Muslims. In 1947, Anees Kidwai's husband, Shafi Ahmed Kidwai (brother of Rafi Ahmed Kidwai), a government servant, was killed in communal violence in Mussoorie because he refused to abandon his post and flee. Devastated by his death, Anees Kidwai took Gandhi's advice and gave herself to social work, working with Partition victims at the Muslim camps in Delhi, at Purana Qila and Humayun's Tomb. Alongside, she kept a diary in which she recorded her experiences and thoughts. This record, published in full only after many years, appeared in Urdu and Hindi under the title, *Azadi Ki Chaon Mein (In the Shadow of Freedom)*.

Translated from the Hindi original by Varsha Das.

Back Again, After 40 Years

RANJIT KAUR

*R*anjit Kaur retired as head mistress of a school in *Srinagar in the early 1980s. Married at the age of 13, she studied upto class VIII in Muzaffarabad in Azad Kashmir, then taught at a local school till she and her family were forced to leave in 1947 and relocate to Srinagar. It was vacation time, she recalls, and the visit to Srinagar was a routine one; but the next day the attacks began and there was no question of returning to Muzaffarabad. Subsequently, the family—and, in fact, the extended community—moved to Jammu; Ranjit Kaur has lived there ever since.*

In 1985 Ranjit Kaur and her husband went back to Muzaffarabad and spent six months there, living with those Hindus and Sikhs, now known as sheikhs, who had converted to Islam and stayed back. Among them were about 25-30 women who had been abducted, converted and married to local Muslims. Ranjit Kaur met all but one of them during her visit, and spoke to them about their experiences: how they had been abducted, where they were taken, how they were treated, and so on. The women were all in purdah, according to her, but no one was prevented from meeting her. Most of them were well-off and well-settled—but she did tell us the story of one woman who killed every child that was born to her of the Muslim Khan who married her forcibly. This was her protest.

Finally, when there was no hope of her being rescued she allowed two children to live.

We met and spoke to her in her house in Jammu in 1992.

> *When you lived in Muzaffarabad, did you have cordial social relations with the Muslims there?*

Oh, yes, we had very friendly relations with them, we would eat and drink with them, but they knew we would eat only dry stuff—sweetmeats, dry fruit—no cooked food... but now, when we were there for five-six months, of course we ate everything. Actually, my attitude had changed earlier, then itself. Because I was a teacher in Srinagar after we came this side, whenever there was a party or school function I would eat openly—in Srinagar there were only Muslims—I wouldn't drink tea but I ate everything else.

> *These five months that you spent there...*

Never mind those five months there, I even ate here, after my promotion, whenever my subordinates invited me, not meat or anything like that, but tea ... made in a different vessel ...

Now, when I was in Muzaffarabad, Sakina said, "Bhenji,"—when they were making tea for everyone and she brought cakes and all for them—she asked, "will you eat this"? And I said, I've always eaten in your house, I'll eat now, too. (*Laughs*) She remembered, you see, but things have changed, now people drink tea and all, but meat ...

All the time we were there they didn't cook meat in our presence.

> *You mean they didn't serve you meat?*

Why would they serve when they knew we wouldn't eat? Not that we're vegetarian but we don't eat halal... only jhatka. So for five months they made vegetables for us, what else? You don't eat anything else, they said, what can we do? You're our guests, but you eat so little you can stay forever and it'll be no burden on us. They didn't even know how to cook dal! But at

Sakina's place and Muzaffar's house, they made very good food. They know how. And very clean, Muzaffar and Sakina put a clean napkin on the bread every day...tea in a flask to our room, and food also. But they didn't eat meat in front of us when we ate together. They showed us great respect.

Whoever invited us, wherever we went to people's houses— the women would tell their husbands, she's here, she's come, go and call her—we would go in the DC's car, to all the small villages also ... people would say, we hear someone has come from India, going around in the DC's car ... (*laughs*). So I would always ask for makki di roti in the villages, always say, you know what we eat, and any milk or lassi or curd, butter... give us these things, that's all.

Only those women who had stayed back (after Partition), who were from here, only they invited us. Usually it was them, but if someone else invited us especially, then we went. Many Muslims also called us ...

You were meeting these women after 40-45 years...how did the conversations begin? What did you say to them?

But they're our own girls, aren't they, we knew them, we could ask them openly: how did you cope? How did you survive, what did you go through? They recognised me, that I was so-and-so's daughter ... some of them had visited us while we were still in Muzaffarabad ...

What did they say, were their men good to them, did they have other wives?

I met many of them, sometimes there may have been other wives also ... but, you know, I met a student of mine there— I used to teach there, too, you know—somebody who knew I used to be a teacher there and I also wanted to meet as many people as I could ... so he said, okay, I'll organise it, there's another family here, too, who stayed back, a Hindu boy who married locally, his family, so I said I would go. It was near Muzaffarabad. So we made a programme, we went one day, stayed there one night, and she told me her story.

She said, "When the attack took place we all gathered together. After they started beating up people we were herded
towards the river ... our men fought back, but they were killed
and they captured us ... and this ancient man, he caught hold
of me and brought me here." She has three or four children
now from him. He also came with her, but as long as he was
present I didn't say anything. What would I say in front of him,
he's a Muslim, after all! But when we went inside we talked
and we talked till two in the morning...she comes and goes to
India, her brother lives in Nagpur, they all know that she's a
Muslim now...but she's alright, no problems in her own home,
her own daughter has been married into a family that converted, sheikh to sheikh, Sikhs who converted and stayed back.
So it's all in the family. But her children are Muslims because
her husband is a Mussalman.

*Did she talk about what happened when she was ab-
ducted?*

Y-e-s, she did, she told me how if they refused to eat beef it
would be put in their mouths at night while they slept...but
then, see, their men will bring them to meet someone from
India if they insist, so... they do respect them. Even with the
men I spoke openly, I wasn't scared of them. When I went to
that small village near Ghori, there were some acquaintances
of ours there also, a woman who had been abducted, a
sheikhni, they took her children away... they brought a Matador to fetch me—they used to run a taxi service—I told them
they would be losing business but they said, no, we'll take
you only, no other passengers... there, next to their house
was another house, a little separate from them, where there
was a young man I knew... Other villagers, Muslims, collected
around to see who had come... so I said, look, you people
used to say in '47, read the *kalma* and become a Muslim, say
la-illa-alillah and you'll be converted. I said how can you believe in all this? I can't accept it. I'll say the *kalma* now, read *la-
illa-laillah* ten times in front of you, tell me does that make me
a Muslim? I'm no Muslim! They just listened. (*Laughs.*)

I told you about that time when this man followed us in his auto as we were going to...you know, I told you, he came behind us and he said, I've come to meet you, said salaam... first he went to where we were staying, to Sakina's, and asked to see us so they told him where we were going...he came alone, and then he told us that he, too, had a sheikhni at home and that she had heard we were visiting and sent him to bring us home to see her. I said, today we're busy, we've already made a programme, but we can come some other time. He said, come tomorrow, so we said fine, we'll come tomorrow. This is how all our meetings were fixed, in advance, that's how it took six months to meet everyone! (*Laughs.*)

So he told us how to reach his house, we said you don't need to come for us, we'll find our way. Will you feed us? You tell me what you want to eat, we'll make it, he said. So we had our fill of lassi and curd and butter, in our own country...

What does Muzaffar do?

Muzaffar? He's a secretary in defence, a very good post in the Secretariat. He's the one who extended our visa... He'll come to India once he retires, can't come now because he won't get a visa. But we had a wonderful visit for six months, did everything to our heart's content in Pakistan.

I didn't meet a single woman there who was unhappy. Of course, they all want to meet their family members, brothers, sisters and all that, but they're quite happy. Even that woman I told you about, who killed all her children as soon as they were born, even she's okay now. Wife of a khan, has children now, is well-off...but she comes here every year or two to meet her brother.

You can see it when you meet them...

Even earlier this was what village life was like, and now it's the same, you survive. These women don't work in the fields, you see...

There's one woman, a sort of relative of mine whom we wanted to meet very badly, we really tried hard, but her husband avoided us, didn't want her to meet us. That DC whose house we went to, he said, don't worry I'll make sure you meet her, this fellow keeps coming to me for lands, so I'll organise it...but he said, it's been so many years and I've known him for so long yet he's never once mentioned that he has a sheikhni in his house. Go and see, and you'll find out whether in fact she's a sheikhni.

So, after about two or three months, he came, came and met us and I said, we want to meet your wife. So he said, you won't be able to find our village, I'll bring her to meet you. But I wanted to see their village, her life there. I didn't tell him that, of course. He said it's a difficult route, the Jeep will not be able to make it for the last few miles, but I said, never mind, we'll do it somehow...

Anyway, he brought her on the day we had fixed but he sat with her throughout, so what could we say? Couldn't talk at all. And he kept her in purdah. Kept sitting with us. So, nothing. Then he said, come tomorrow, come to the house we're staying at. So we went, they had cooked for us, and I got an opportunity to talk to her in the kitchen. The men couldn't come there. And there I asked her, I said, tell me, have you never stepped outside the house even to fetch water—their village is in the interior—or to go to a wedding or a funeral? And she said, no, never, he goes on his own. Doesn't let me go anywhere. Complete seclusion. And why do I need to go for water, I've never even fetched one lota of water, the servants get it...

You see, our relative's son was a minister there and he filed a report against him, kept sending the police to his house, so he was afraid they would take her away. Wouldn't let her out of the house. After the report was filed he became even stricter, wouldn't tell anyone about her. That's why the DC said he wasn't sure she was there at all. Anyway, now she has children, now how can she come away? She wants to come, meet her family, but... Her sister went to see her, all of them went, tried to bring her, but no.

Now this Khan's wife who killed all her children, she took us everywhere, made sure we met people, brought a Matador, the driver was also a sheikh, and she accompanied us. She introduced us to many Sardars who had stayed back.

How did you feel, returning after so many years?

Oh, it's changed a lot, Muzaffarabad. The streets are the same, the old ones, but where there were open fields there are buildings now. But Muzaffar's house is the same. I mean they've added a few rooms on top, but otherwise... the family's well settled, all the brothers are doing well.

Our house, my parent's house, was in the city and there's a doctor living in it now. He heard we were visiting so he called us over. Gave us tea and we saw our old house, it was just the same. The doctor said he was building his own house near the Secretariat and then this would be vacant. You can take it, he said, I'll hand over the keys to you. I laughed and said, what will we do with it now. If we lived here, we'd take it. No, no, you do whatever you like with it, sell it, do what you want...I said, we didn't come here for that, for people to say they've come to claim their property, will they ever trust us again? (*Half-laughs, half-cries.*) Even after we came away he sent a message saying the house is yours. Such a nice man. I thought then, Sakina doesn't have a home of her own, why doesn't he give it to her! (*Laughs.*) Let her live in it, she's done so much for us...I really thought hard about it, but then I realised it would be very tricky, difficult for Sakina...

Did you ever get a chance to talk to the men who converted, the men who became sheikhs?

They weren't men then when we left, they were just boys, they're men now, and they all married sheikhnis, not Muslims, except that one who took me to Mansera...No grown men were spared you see, they were all killed. I mean, they killed the Sikhs and the Sikhs killed them. That's why there's so much hatred in their hearts for them...

— *Interviewed by Kamla Bhasin and Ritu Menon*

Jatin & Ismat

KAMLABEN PATEL

The loss of lives and property, and the widespread violence that accompanied Partition have been well documented by historians and scholars of Independence. Less well-known is the incidence of the large-scale abduction of women of all three communities, Hindu, Muslim and Sikh, during that period. No official estimates exist of the exact number of such abductions, but it is safe to assume that there would have been well over 1,00,000 or more. In the aftermath of Partition, the governments of India and Pakistan were swamped with complaints by the relatives of 'missing' women, seeking to recover them either through government, military or voluntary efforts. Recognizing the enormity of the problem, the two governments entered into an Inter-Dominion Agreement in November 1947 to recover as many women as possible, as speedily as possible, from each country and restore them to their families.

In all, approximately 30,000 women—12,000 Muslim and 18,000 non-Muslim—were recovered by the police and social workers of both countries, primarily between 1947 and 1952. Kamlaben Patel, an Indian social worker, was stationed in Lahore for a few years and was actively involved in recovering Hindu and Sikh women from Pakistan. Recovery work had been entrusted to the Women's Section, Ministry of Relief and Rehabilitation, under the direction of two principal honorary advisers, Rameshwari Nehru and Mridula Sarabhai. Kamlaben

Patel, a Gandhian, was Mridula Sarabhai's right-hand woman till 1952, and represented both India and Pakistan on the Special Tribunals set up by both governments, to resolve disputed cases. The following accounts are excerpted from her book, Mool Soota Ukhadela (*Torn from the Roots*).

I n the days before Partition, there was a reputed Pathan family in Rawalpindi who used to go to Kashmir every year for a vacation. Similarly, a Hindu businessman from Amritsar and his family also went to Kashmir for their holidays. Both stayed at the same hotel and mixed freely with one another. Their families became very friendly, and at the end of each vacation, expressed the desire to meet again the next year at the same place. This practice continued till Partition. Lalaji had a son whose name was Jatin, and the younger daughter of the Pathan family was called Ismat. Without really being aware of it Jatin and Ismat fell in love—Jatin was nineteen and Ismat, sixteen.

Within a few days of Partition, Pakistan had sent raiders into the Kashmir valley and they started making sporadic attacks in the region. The district of Rawalpindi was adjacent to the Kashmir border, and in those days there was only one overland route to Kashmir, through Rawalpindi. As such, Rawalpindi was an important strategic town for Pakistan for the raiders to infiltrate. There had been a massacre of Indians in this area and temporary camps were set up to facilitate the migration of the Hindus. They were overcrowded with refugees. Young Ismat couldn't understand all this but one thing was clear to her, that from now on it would not be possible for her to go to Kashmir. Meeting Jatin was out of the question. Faced with this reality her dormant feelings for Jatin surfaced and she became anxious. She did not have an address for Jatin—all she knew was that he and his family lived in Amritsar. With childlike impulsiveness she made up her mind to reach Amritsar at any cost, to meet him. She then began to explore various

possibilities for getting there. Very soon she got the opportunity she was looking for. One day, when her father had gone
to Peshawar to attend to some business and her mother had
retired to bed early because of ill health, Ismat decided to take
advantage of the situation. She packed a few essentials in a
small bag and, with the promise of a suitable reward, coaxed a
servant to accompany her to the refugee camp which was about
a kilometre away. She left home at about 8 pm.

It was a month after Partition and the refugee camp was
very crowded. Trains plied between Rawalpindi and Amritsar,
carrying refugees to India. The Indian army was in charge of
the camp. Boldly Ismat approached the Camp Commander and
said, "I am a Hindu girl separated from my parents. Please make
immediate arrangements to have me sent to India." Looking at
her, the Commander saw the danger in letting this young girl
stay at the camp for any length of time, and so he took her in
his jeep to Rawalpindi station and saw her off on a train bound
for Amritsar.

A number of volunteers and workers used to be present at
Amritsar railway station to prepare lists of incoming refugees
and to give them much-needed information and guidance when
they arrived. As soon as a train came in from Pakistan, a number
of people flocked to the station to inquire about their kith and
kin who had been left behind in Pakistan. The unfortunate
refugees who alighted from the trains, having left all ther
worldly belongings, their homes and property, and having
come through numerous traumatic experiences, always heaved
a sigh of relief as they set foot on Indian soil. But the very next
moment, reminded of their immense loss, of the family and
assets left behind, they would begin crying and wailing. Volunteers and workers who had been working there round the
clock soon grew familiar with these outbursts.

When Ismat alighted from the train, her face did not reveal
the slightest trace of misery or trauma. On the contrary it was
bright and glowing with excitement, as she saw her plan succeed. She possessed a beautiful figure which distinguised her

from the other passengers. After getting off the train she walked to one corner of the platform and patiently waited there with her small suitcase. Very soon the attention of a volunteer was drawn to her. Those days Mr Bhimsen Sachar (who became Chief Minister of East Punjab and later Governor of Andhra Pradesh) and Mrs Sachar were often present at the railway station when refugee trains came in from Pakistan. They came there to give solace to the refugees and look after their needs. The volunteer led Ismat to the Sachars. Mr Sachar asked her a few questions in response to which she repeated the story she had fabricated. She said she belonged to a village near Rawalpindi where she lived with her parents. At the time of Partition she was visiting a maternal aunt in a nearby village. Before she could return home the riots broke out and her aunt forbade her from leaving. It was with great difficulty that she had been able to reach the refugee camp, she said. At the camp she learnt that her parents had already reached India. Those days, in Punjab, the language, dress and manner of both Hindus and Muslims were very similar, so there was little reason for anyone to disbelieve her story or to suspect that she was not, as she claimed, a Hindu. Mr Sachar instructed a responsible woman worker to take special care of her and make arrangements to send her to the refugee camp.

During the course of her conversation with local workers at the camp, Ismat not only manged to obtain Jatin's address but also sent him a message to come and take her away. Jatin arrived and spoke to her, but she was not allowed to leave the camp with him as she was legally still a minor. However, he and his parents managed to get the necessary permission from the District Commissioner to take Ismat away. The camp incharge was then left with no alternative but to hand the girl over to them. Jatin's family gave their consent to the marriage and before our volunteers could get a stay order from the court, they were married in the premises of the Golden Temple in Amritsar. They began to lead a happy married life.

Now, India and Pakistan had entered into an agreement to recover women abducted during the Partition riots in the two countries. At a cabinet level meeting of the two Dominions, the Rehabilitation Minister of Pakistan himself requested his Indian counterpart, Shri Gopalaswamy Iyengar, to recover Ismat from India. Mridulaben and I were present at the meeting when this request was made and we knew which case he was referring to, but we remained silent at the time. Shri Iyengar promised the Pakistan minister that a proper investigation would be done and necessary action taken. (Later, this case came up for discussion at the Search Service Bureau in Amritsar, which was entrusted with the task of recovering abducted women.) Eventually the news also reached Jatin who was keeping a close watch on developments, and also on my visits to Amritsar. When I was there next he heard of my arrival and immediately rushed to our office to see me. He narrated the whole story to me in an effort to convince me that it was not a case of abduction at all because Ismat had come to India voluntarily. I suggested to him that he meet Mridulaben, but he was not prepared to do so. In those days Mridulaben was highly respected in Punjab, but at the same time people were sometimes afraid of her because of her strict and disciplinarian ways. Even high-ranking officials of the Punjab government were in awe of her. They often avoided direct interaction with her and preferred to go through me. I explained to Jatin that since the case had been taken up at the Inter-Dominion level it was unlikely that I could be of much help.

At the next Inter-Dominion meeting in Lahore this case was discussed. Returning from the meeting, Mridulaben took a lift with the Secretary and I was in the Service Bureau car with K.L. Punjabi and Nagpal. The idea of sending Ismat back to Pakistan did not find favour with me or Nagpal; I asked K.L. Punjabi why they considered this to be a case of abduction when Ismat had travelled such a long way under such gruelling circumstances to come over to Amritsar. Moreover, how could the Indian government hand her over to Pakistan against her will? Shri Punjabi said that since the case involved a minor Muslim girl and a Hindu boy, it would be difficult to convince the girl's parents to drop the charges. If the situation was reversed and it was a young Hindu girl, would we be prepared to let her go without making any effort to recover her? The Pakistan government also would not take kindly to it, and it would become even more difficult to enforce the agreement to hand over recovered Hindu women if we failed to send Ismat back. It was important to keep the public interest in mind rather than be swayed by emotion. This gave me an indication of the stand the Indian government would take on this and similar cases.

After some time Shri Kaliprasadji went to Jatin's residence and persuaded both Ismat and him to come to Hotel Amritsar to meet Mridulaben. Mridulaben's patience was sorely tried as she tried to deal with Ismat. She even offered to accompany her across the Wagah border to meet her parents. But Ismat would not agree to this proposal. Leaving Mridulaben's office she told me, "It is immaterial whether Mridulaben accompanies me to the border or god himself comes with me. As soon as my parents see me they will kill me. I am not prepared to meet them under any circumstances."

After this meeting with Mridulaben, Jatin became apprehensive that the police would come and take Ismat away forcibly, so both of them fled to Calcutta. We could not get any information regarding their whereabouts, either from their families or from their neighbours. Meanwhile the pressure from the Pakistan government to recover the girl kept mounting. We, the workers, reported that we had already done all in our power to recover the girl and could do no more—as far as we were concerned the case was closed.

I believe that when Ismat and Jatin heard that the case was now closed, they returned to Amritsar to plan their strategy to satisfy Ismat's parents.

One of Ismat's maternal uncles was in the External Affairs Ministry in Pakistan, so we sent him a message and requested him to come to Delhi to discuss the case. When he arrived we arranged a meeting between him and Ismat. It took nearly four or five days to persuade her to go with her uncle to meet her parents in Lahore. In the meantime we called Mr Rizvi, the Superintendent of Police in charge of recovering women from West Punjab, from Lahore. After much cajoling and coaxing it was agreed that Ismat would go to Lahore with Mr Rizvi and her uncle. She would stay there as a guest of the Inspector General of Police, Khan Qurban Ali Khan. During this period her parents could meet her, and at the end of seven days she would give her final decision in the presence of her parents. Jatin, as well as all of us, would abide by her decision.

Mridulaben entrusted me with the task of helping them cross the border without trouble or humiliation. One fine morning I received information that Ismat and her escorts were scheduled to leave Delhi by the afternoon flight, and I was expected to receive them at Amritsar airport and go with them to Lahore.

I left Lahore at noon and reached our office at Amritsar Hotel, from where Shri Kaliprasadji joined me on my way to the airport. We were hopeful that we would reach Lahore before dark.

Ismat, Jatin, Ismat's uncle and Mr Rizvi disembarked from the plane. Ismat was loaded with gold ornaments, and I gathered from their converasation that there were more in her bag. I knew that all these ornaments were given to her by Jatin and his parents. I hinted to Jatin that it was neither wise nor safe to carry such valuables across the border, but he paid no attention to my words and allowed Ismat to take them with her if she wanted. I was certain that the customs officers at the Border Check Post would object, but they did not conduct any search. They simply said, "Madam, we know you very well. There is no need to search your car, you can go." It was apparent that they recognised my car because of my frequent trips between Lahore and Amritsar. I was taken aback, but in the presence of a shrewd and experienced police officer like Mr

Rizvi, I was left with no alternative but to smile and thank the customs officials for their courtesy!

After reaching Lahore we proceeded to the Pakistan government's secretariat where we were to hand Ismat over to Khan Qurban Ali Khan. But Ismat refused to get down from the car and insisted that she would go there only if Jatin accompanied her and stayed with her. When Mr Rizvi tried to explain to her that it was inadvisable to risk alienating her parents further, Ismat countered by saying that Jatin could hide in the next room when her parents arrived. After more than an hour of persuasion Jatin finally convinced her to go to her parents, saying that he would see her after seven days anyway. She was then taken to Khan Qurban Ali's residence, along with her maternal uncle and Mr Rizvi.

When I got back to the camp at Gangaram Hospital my colleagues asked where I had disappeared to so suddenly. Jokingly, I replied that I had gone to receive Romeo and Juliet! That night we had an interesting gossip session in my room. Jatin related his story to everyone. We felt that it was not safe for him to remain in Lahore for this protracted period and suggested that he leave for Amritsar and return after six days. Before leaving he tried to contact Ismat on phone, but in vain. He was informed that she had gone out shopping. Reluctantly, he left for Amritsar.

We were all anxiously waiting for the seven days to end. In the meantime Mridulaben arrived in Lahore four days later. The day she came we had to attend a meeting with Pakistani officials. The meeting ended earlier than expected so we had some time to spare. Mridulaben expressed a desire to meet Ismat. On inquiring we were told that she had gone to her father's place. We were rather surprised to hear this. It now seemed imperative that we should meet her, so we got her father's address and went there. On reaching the house we sent word to the zenana about our arrival. After a long wait her *abba* entered the sitting room. His manner towards us was indifferent. After some hesitation he called Ismat. When we

saw her we could not believe our eyes. She had changed completely. Her clothes, manner and behaviour were transformed—
we thought she was Ismat's sister so different did she seem!
Even the expression on her face had changed. Pointing a finger at Mridulaben and addressing her mother she said, "That
woman with short hair is the culprit! She prevented me from
coming here. I requested her repeatedly but she paid no heed
and detained me all this while." We were dumbstruck. It was a
very disturbing situation for us and even more so for me. With
great difficulty I managed to control my temper and asked her,
"What about the promises you made to us when we parted
company near the Secretariat? You agreed to give your final
decision in Jatin's presence. Do you recall that?"

Hearing Jatin's name Ismat flared up and shouted, "I never
want to see that rascal's face. I wish I could cut him into pieces
and throw him to the dogs!" We realized it was pointless staying there any longer. As we were ushered out of the house
Mridulaben appeared to be rather preoccupied. I grew nervous thinking about what I would tell Jatin. I had been so
shocked by our meeting that it did not even strike me to ask
Ismat to return the ornaments given to her by Jatin's family. I
felt we had lost a valuable opportunity. We narrated this incident to Shri Nagpal at the camp, who consoled me by saying
that he himself would go to Amritsar and explain the situation
to Jatin and his family. I was very relieved.

This work of recovering abducted women was telling on
our nerves. We were always under a terrible strain, taking one
blow after another. This latest one was the most severe. It had
so shaken my entire being that even as I write these lines today, I feel I have not been able to recover from it completely.
As there were a number of pressing problems we had no alternative but to devote our attention to them. Slowly we started
to get over the incident.

Three days later Jatin arrived and confronted me. It pained
me to see his face. He was furious. "You have betrayed me.
Ismat promised to give her final decision in my presence

today. Take me to her now. I want to hear her decision myself. I don't trust anyone anymore."

When all my efforts to pacify him failed, I telephoned the officer who had acted as the mediator and requested him to arrange a meeting between the two. But the experienced fellow replied that Ismat and her family had already left Lahore. Further, he said, I should make sure that Jatin did not visit Lahore again because it would be unsafe for him to do so.

Jatin was not prepared to listen to me at all. He couldn't believe that Ismat had said those things. He was sure she had been under pressure from her parents and that she would certainly change her stand on seeing him.

"You should have taken me with you. Why did you go without me?"he asked us over and over agin. The next day, after a great deal of persuasion, we managed to send him back to Amritsar with somebody.

In those days a bus used to travel from Lahore to Amritsar every day, carrying refugees. It would leave from our Lahore office. Once I spotted Jatin in the queue, buying a ticket. I asked him the purpose of his visit. He replied that he had come to Lahore a couple of days earlier and was trying to gather information about Ismat's whereabouts. He was determined to contact her at any cost, determined to hear her decision from her own lips. He would not give up till he had done so.

I tried my best to tell him that it was not advisable or safe for him to stay in Lahore, but he turned a deaf ear to my pleas, saying, "I am totally ruined already, why should I be afraid of dying?"

I felt very sorry for him but knew it was pointless expressing my sympathy, so I assured him that I would do my best to gather the information that he wanted. I also asked him not to come to Lahore until I had something for him. He however refused to give me any such assurance. He was still very angry. Though he had talked to me he was completely unprepared to speak to Mridulaben.

During the course of my next visit to Amritsar I made it a point to visit Jatin's mother. She, too, was extremely unhappy about her son's anguish. She seized the opportunity to do some plain talking. She asked me to recover the ornaments that had been given to Ismat. I promised her I'd do the best I could, and asked her to see to it that her son did not visit Lahore again.

I was indeed anxious to get some news about Ismat and, under the pretext of asking about the ornaments again, contacted the Pakistani police officer who had mediated on the case. But he simply brushed aside my request and advised me, in a polite formal way, that Ismat and her family had left Lahore long back, but that he would talk to them about the ornaments if he got an opportunity in the future. With these words he put a full stop to the whole matter. I could say nothing more. I knew I would get no help from him.

After that I saw Jatin in Lahore a couple of times, but he avoided me. I learnt from his mother that he was squandering a lot of money in his efforts to trace Ismat. In 1952 I met Jatin again as I was travelling from Delhi to Bombay by the Frontier Mail. He was going to Bombay to see a cricket match. His face was pale and he looked emaciated. His companion confided to me that he was suffering from TB. He was behaving very irresponsibly, despite warnings and medical advice to take complete rest. I was very sorry to hear this but was unable to muster the courage to give him any more advice.

Lock Up Your Hearts

KAMLABEN PATEL

The district of Mianwali is situated on the border of the Punjab adjoining the North West Frontier Province. It is the last district of the Punjab towards the west. The setting up of a camp for the recovery of abducted women was comparatively difficult in this district. Cases of abduction were quite frequent in that district even before Partition. In view of these conditions, a middle aged, khadi-clad lady was sent there to manage the work of the camp. She possessed the necessary zeal and ability to pursue this work, yet the work was at a virtual standstill. Lists of abducted women were routinely given to the Pakistani police but they were usually returned, marked with 'not traceable' against most names. Though it was apparent that the police were evading the work, it was impossible to take action against them. Fed up with this attitude, the lady in charge of the camp undertook a protest fast. Our army unit in Mianwali district relayed this news to me via the wireless network. I didn't consider this a proper thing to do and so I sought Mridulaben's advice on the matter. After consulting other high-ranking officers and Mrs Rameshwari Nehru, I was instructed, by phone, to travel to Mianwali at the earliest and persuade the lady to abandon her fast. Besides this I was also supposed to discuss and sort out the recovery work with the local officers.

I left for Mianwali the next day accompanied by a police escort. I reached there in the evening after a long journey. With great difficulty I persuaded the mataji to give up her fast and eat some food. It was her third day of fasting. I invited her to visit Lahore and she agreed to do so.

Next day a meeting of local police officers was convened and we discussed matters pertaining to recovery work. After the meeting was over, one of the police officers offered to take me on a sight-seeing tour. I gladly accepted, knowing from past experience how important it was to build a rapport with officers of the other country, and how this had always helped me in my work. The officer who showed me around had relatives in Bombay and he, too, used to visit Bombay in the vacations. In the course of our conversation we discovered we had a lot of common things to talk about. On our way back he showed me a well and said, "A number of women from this locality committed suicide by jumping into this well to avoid being raped and molested. At one time the well was almost full to the brim with dead bodies. It is strange that you have come all the way from Bombay to recover abducted women at considerable risk to your own life, but we who live here have not been able to protect the women of our own locality. And as if this is not enough, we have compounded it by abducting the mothers and sisters of our fellow human beings. How sternly will posterity judge us?"

As he said this his voice quivered and the corners of his eyes became moist. I glimpsed the sensitive heart that hid beneath the stiff exterior of a police uniform. At first I presumed he was from UP or Bihar, a refugee, and therefore so sympathetic to our cause, but inquiries revealed that he was a native of Punjab. He had not sustained any personal loss during the course of these turbulent years, but in the town where he was born and brought up there had been many Hindus who were his childhood friends and companions. He had helped many of them reach the safety of refugee camps and migrate to India. He had even acted as custodian of the valuables his friends left behind. He then added, "After the departure of my companions I feel lonely, though I am living in the midst of my own community."

Over the years I came into contact with so many officers in connection with my work and each of them left a distinct impression on my mind. But while I have forgotten most of them, the agony I saw on the face of this man has stayed with me for a long time.

On my way back from Mianwali I was scheduled to make a brief stop at Sargodha to discuss the speeding up of recovery work with local officers. As the discussions took longer than expected, and it became dark, we decided to spend the night there. The next day, before we left, the Pakistan police brought a child aged about four to the camp. He appeared to be in deep shock. His eyes were swollen with constant crying and his voice had become hoarse. He didn't stop crying even after we offered him sweets and toys. To all our questions he just shook his head, refusing to utter a word. Finally it was unanimously decided that I should take the child to the Lahore camp. We thought that seeing other children there might help him become normal. When we got into the car he appeared to be happy for a short while and then resumed his crying. During the eight hour journey he didn't stop crying except for a few spells of intermittent sleep.

I handed him over to the camp-in-charge after getting back and then, because of the intense pressure of work, forgot about him. After about three days the camp-in-charge reported to me that the boy appeared to be Muslim. She said, "He calls himself Latif but doesn't know the names of his parents. He plays with the other children but his manner and behaviour indicate that he is not Hindu."

It was unlikely that a mistake had been made because it was the Pakistani police who had brought him to our camp. I suggested therefore that we shouldn't be in a hurry to transfer him to the Jalandar camp but keep him with us for a few more days.

In the meantime his so-called grandparents arrived at the camp from Sargodha. We called Latif to the office to meet them. As soon as he saw them tears began to fall from all three pairs of eyes.

Latif's grandfather said, "Latif is our daughter's son. His mother passed away when he was very young. He has been with us since. After his mother died his father did not bother to inquire about him. His mother was our only child and we are spending our last years bringing up our grandson."

We were convinced of the veracity of the story but couldn't restore him to them without the permission of the Pakistani authorities. This was in accordance with the Indo-Pak agreement. I tried to explain this to them, "We are sorry we cannot restore him to you. This case will be put up before the Tribunal. You should represent your case before them, and if the members are convinced that he is your grandson we will certainly hand him over to you."

We didn't agree to their request that Latif's Muslim grandmother stay with him in the camp as this was against the rules. They could stay elsewhere in Lahore and come to the camp every day to meet their grandson.

When the case came up before the Tribunal, Latif's grandparents were present. They represented their case but the members did not accept their version. Besides, Latif's name was nowhere on our list of abducted persons. The police of Sargodha had, on their own, brought him to our camp. The Tribunal members were of the opinion that the Pakistani police could not have made such a mistake. The case was adjourned for the next sitting and it was decided to summon the Sargodha police for the hearing.

All of us were astounded when the Sargodha police submitted their statement. Latif's grandparents were called in for cross-examination and finally the real story emerged.

The old couple had had only one daughter. She had no child even after being married for many years. In her neighbourhood there lived a Hindu artisan who had three children.

The old couple's daughter loved the youngest child of the Hindu neighbour and kept him with her most of the time. The child was cute and healthy. When he was hardly two years old, his father passed away leaving his mother with the responsibility of bringing up three children. The widow found it increasingly difficult to support and maintain the family, so the youngest child began to spend more and more time with his Muslim foster mother who was keen to keep him with her. When communal riots broke out in Punjab, the minority community panicked and started fleeing their homes to places of safety. "Latif's mother got ready to go to the Hindu refugee camp along with her Hindu neighbours. Before leaving she said to her Muslim neighbour, "I feel I should leave Latif with you. You have brought him up and he, too, has a strong attachment to you. I don't know where I will go and what our fate will be. If we find a place I will come back to get Latif. In case I don't turn up, I am sure you will bring him up like your own son." The child did not feel the loss of his real mother and began to live happily with his foster mother, whom he had always regarded as his real mother anyway. But fate willed otherwise for Latif. After about six months the foster mother took him along to meet her parents. Unfortunately, while she was there she died of pneumonia. On her deathbed she handed Latif over to her parents and said, "It is my last wish that you should treat Latif as if he was my own son, and make him heir to all the property I would have inherited."

And so the old couple brought up the child with care and affection. With the passing of time their attachment to him also increased and his company helped ease their grief over the death of their daughter. The old man had a house and a piece of land. His brother and nephews began to resent Latif because he would inherit the property. When the law for the recovery of abducted women and children came into effect, they saw an opportunity to get rid of Latif. They reported the matter to the police and convinced them that Latif should be sent to India as he was a Hindu boy. It was at their instigation that the police brought him to our camp at Sargodha.

Now the whole case was crystal clear. It proved beyond doubt that Latif was a Hindu and therefore there was no alternative but to send him to India. Latif's 'grandparents' stared at me in mute appeal. He was sitting in his grandmother's lap with his arms around her neck. I was deeply moved by this sight. I failed to understand what gave us the right to deprive this child of the affection and care his foster grandparents were willing to give him. No one knew where his real mother was or whether she was alive. Nobody even knew her full name. How would we trace her? And if we didn't find her what would happen to this poor child? He would be brought up in the camp environment, deprived of love and affection. I was moved to tears at the thought of his future. I requested the Tribunal to postpone their verdict to the next sitting. But there was no ground on which they could concede my request. It had been proved without a doubt that Latif was Hindu. Seeing my agonised expression one of the members of the Tribunal addressed me politely, " You should not be swept away by emotion. We have to take a decision in accordance with the agreement entered into by both Dominions."

I controlled myself and replied, "That is true. But it would not be a violation of the agreement if the decision were withheld for some time."

Finally the Tribunal conceded my request and the decision was postponed. They then took up other cases, but I could scarcely apply my mind to them as a great conflict was raging within me. Why should I be party to a decision in which an innocent young boy was being uprooted from affectionate care and a secure life to be thrust into the insecurity and uncertainty of camp life? After careful consideration his own mother had handed over custody of the child to this family. He had not been abducted or taken forcibly. How did anyone have the right to snatch the child from that family? The demand for Partition was made by Jinnah to inflate his own ego, and the

Muslim League backed it to enhance its own political importance. The Congress had had no option but to agree. Neither
the Congress nor the Muslim League had any idea about the
dire consequences that would follow their decision—it was
ordinary people who had to take the traumatic consequences.
Millions of lives were shattered, so many had died and others
who had survived were no better than the dead. The refugee
camps were no better than pig-stys, overcrowded and filthy.
There was inadequate sanitation and several contagious dis-
eases were spreading, taking the death toll higher as a result.
It was proving difficult to provide refugees with the basic minimum of food and clothes. Under such circumstances it was
foolish to think that arrangements could be made to resettle
and rehabilitate them in India. During the riots that followed
Partition, thousands of women were abducted and taken away
as if they were commodities. Later, both Dominions entered
into an agreement to recover these women and children, and
specific rules were framed to handle the cases. But nowhere
in those rules was there any provision made for the recovered
women and children to decide their own futures. And we, the
so-called social workers, were engaged in transferring them
from one country to the other under the mistaken idea that we
were doing noble and humanitarian work! The shackles of rules
and regulations had become such a routine matter that they
had stopped affecting us any more. But a case like this once
again made me aware of the inhumanity of enforcing rules
blindly and unthinkingly. Still, despite much soul-searching, I
was unable to decide to what extent individual freedom could
be curbed in the larger interests of society.

After the session was over I rose mechanically, returned to
my quarters and threw myself on the bed. I had lost my appetite and sleep. My mind was torn between these conflicting
ideas, and I wondered why I should continue with this work
any more. I could not decide whether the real object of helping abducted women and children was served or not. I was
inclined to feel more and more that we had not succeeded in

our mission of helping abducted women, because we could not generate in them the awareness that we were their well-wishers. The unimaginable tragedy that they had been subjected to had rendered them incapable of deciding what was good or bad for them. Under such circumstances I felt as if all our efforts and the risks undertaken by us were an exercise in futility. On the other hand I felt that we had been able to help in a few cases and alleviate the suffering of some women. Since much still remained to be done it would be cowardice on my part to abandon the work at this juncture. I found myself facing a dilemma and wondered why women had remained in such a state of helplessness. How long would they have to depend on men for their protection? Was it true that men were physically stronger than women? Did women's innate strength have no value vis-à-vis a man's physical strength?

...Haunted by these thoughts I fell asleep. But when I awoke, Latif's case popped up once again. How could I save that unlucky child?

...Two options were open to me. The first was to keep Latif at the Lahore camp till his mother was traced in India, and the other was to hand him over to his foster grandparents through the Sargodha police till the arrival of his mother. I took the Indian member of the Tribunal into confidence. Before the session started I took him aside and proposed the first alternative to him. He did not like my suggestion. The gist of his argument was: "It might set a bad precedent. Latif is undoubtedly a Hindu boy, he has to go to India regardless of whether his mother is traceable or not. There are hundreds of such children in India, and one more will make no difference. I fail to understand your logic in keeping him here at the Lahore camp."

I tried again, "Once we send him to Jalandar the police will slacken in their efforts to find his mother. If he stays here they will be under pressure."

Just to oblige me the member conceded my request but warned me, "I request you to put your emotions away when you come to the next sitting of the Tribunal."

My rejoinder to him was, "You must not forget that I have been deputed by the government to the Tribunal because you people leave your hearts locked up at home."

As soon as the sitting began I submitted my proposal, and it was accepted without much discussion. I asked the camp-in-charge to explain the decision to Latif's foster grandparents and tell them to return home...

The old couple walked back, crying bitterly. Latif adjusted to our company and life in the camp. He was a loveable child and everybody liked him. Every morning he used to come to my room. After a few days he started saying 'namaskar' to us instead of 'salaam'. My old ayah grew very fond of him.

Passing through the bazaar one day I saw a baby suit in a shop window. Instantly I asked the driver, Shyam Singh, to buy it for Latif. It fitted him very well and he was overjoyed when he wore it. From that day on he was affectionately called "Behenji's child". I tried to detach myself from him as much as I could but he used to visit my room constantly. Whenever he saw me go out he would hug me affectionately. One day, as I was about to get into the car to go to the Mall Road office, I saw him sitting with Shyam Singh. I looked at Shyam Singh questioningly and he said, "He wants to sit in the car. After all he is a child. Let him come with us—I'll take care of him." I nodded. Latif was thrilled. My ayah suggested that it was not right to call him Latif—he should be given another name to suit his changed situation.

The Tribunal held its next meeting. Latif's mother had still not been traced. I, too, was impatiently awaiting the final decision on his case because he had become extremely attached to us. Under the circumstances it was not desirable that he stay on in the camp.

On the appointed date the Tribunal met again. I had spent the previous night tossing restlessly in bed. I knew the only solution was to send him to the Jalandar camp but my heart would not accept this. I was unable to decide what course to take. What was best for him? Suppose we sent him with his foster grandparents, not only was it against the rules, what would happen to him once the old couple passed away? He would be at the mercy of the other relatives who would not let him inherit the property. By that time, most likely, the Recovery Organisation, too, would have wound up and he would lose his right to migrate to India. As a converted Muslim he would constantly be persecuted. On the other hand living in the Jalandar camp with other orphan children might not be the best thing either. The only silver lining was a chance that some kind person might adopt him and then his future prospects would improve. He could then even get a job on a priority basis as a refugee.

The next morning when my ayah brought me bed tea she looked at my face and remarked, " You appear to have had a sleepless night. Why do you worry so much? Why don't you' adopt Latif?" I told her not to waste my time talking nonsense, and added that I could not bring up a child nor did I have the resources to settle him in future. But the ayah's lightly made suggestion made me think.

Punjabis have a fetish about adopting children. Despite having their own, they seem to be ever ready to take on another if they come across a healthy, good-looking baby. I recollected that when about 40 Hindu children from Bannu who had survived the massacre on the Gujarat train, had been brought to our camp, many refugees requested me to let them adopt the children. Whenever I visited Delhi, a Punjabi telephone operator at Constitution House would invariably request me to get him a healthy baby for adoption. Once I inquired if he had any children of his own, and he replied that he had two but since they were now grown up he wanted an infant that he and his wife could look after and spend their time with.

According to the rules we were not allowed to hand over the recovered women and children to their relatives either at Lahore or at any of the camps set up in Pakistan. They could ɒe handed over only at Jalandar in the presence of a magistrate. The reason for this was that in the beginning many distant relatives had taken away such women and children. I was relieved to know that Latif would be given to a well-to-do family for adoption in case his mother was not traced after another six months at the Jalandar camp. The Tribunal met again and discussed Latif's case once more. Looking at me the Indian member proposed that, though efforts to trace Latif's mother were still in progress, it was time he was sent to India. His case was closed on our files. When I nodded my consent, both members of the Tribunal were rather surprised.

I suggested that his foster grandparents be informed that Latif would henceforth be in Jalandar. I did not want to see their sad faces and therefore avoided telling them myself. Listening to stories of misery and suffering from morning to evening, day after day, made me want to avoid meeting them.

Soon preparations began to send Latif to Jalandar. His joy knew no bounds when the ayah, the driver and my colleagues presented him with toys, biscuits, etc. He happily boarded the vehicle which was to carry the recovered women to Jalandar. Cheerfully he bade us farewell.

Mrs Krishna Thapar, who was the camp-in-charge at Jalandar was a nice person and I was friendly with her. I sent her a message to take special care of Latif, and that I would discuss his case with her in detail when I next visited Jalandar.

Abandoned

KAMLABEN PATEL

In times of war a number of illegitimate children are born as a result of extra-marital relations. These children are called war babies, and the government of the country where they are born is held responsible for their upkeep. Such children are usually with their mothers, since the whereabouts of their fathers are often unknown. A large number of women were abducted from India and Pakistan during the turbulent days of Partition. In fact abductions had taken place even before, as early as March 1947, when communal disturbances had broken out in erstwhile undivided Punjab. It was around December, 1949, that an organisation was set up for recovering abducted women. In the beginning a problem arose as to what was to be done about those children who were born after Partition. After a lot of discussion it was finally decided that the recovered women be allowed to leave their children in the custody of their fathers before leaving the country where the children were born. To Pakistani authorities it did not matter much whether Muslim women returned to Pakistan along with their children or not, but for the government of India it was a complex problem. In Indian society a child born to a Hindu mother by a Muslim father was hardly acceptable, and if the relatives of the women did not accept such women and their children, the problem of rehabilitation would be huge. It would be impossible to find suitable matches for the young recovered women with the added liability of children. Considering all aspects of the problem, social workers engaged in this work were of the opinion that it would be wise to leave these children behind with their fathers instead of allowing their mothers to bring them over to India, where eventually such children were likely to end up in orphanages. A meeting of the persons concerned was convened in Delhi to take a final decision in this matter. I was invited from Lahore to attend. On the face of it, such a solution appeared to be the right one, but thinking over the problem I shuddered at the prospect of the actions we would be required to take to force recovered women to abandon their children. I could not bear the idea of separating an infant from its mother. It was extremely difficult for us to find the proper words to console the recovered women.

In the meeting, I raised this point as a representative of the social workers actually associated with the work of recovery. The Joint Secretary in the Ministry of Recovery and Rehabilitation was a senior and seasoned civil servant. He firmly believed that this was the only practical solution and there was no need to be blinded by emotions while arriving at a decision. I mustered my courage and said, "The soldiers responsible for their birth go back to their respective countries and the infants have to be brought up by their mothers. Nobody separates them from their mothers. Stalwarts and seasoned social workers like Rameshwari Nehru should therefore visit Lahore and impart necessary training for separating the child. On our part we have neither the strength nor the capability for that work. If all of you do not approve of my suggestion I would like to disassociate myself from this work." The issue was discussed at length at other meetings, too. Finally it was decided that recovered Hindu women should be given an option to leave their children behind in Pakistan, or bring them to India. It was decided that even after coming to India, if a mother desired to leave her child she could do so in Amritsar. It was further decided to make adequate arrangements to bring up such infants. It was our experience that a few Hindu women

who were mothers of two or three children did finally agree
with a heavy heart to leave their children behind, but most
unmarried young women were not willing to part with their
children. Social workers tried very hard to persuade them that
it was in their own interest, as well as that of the infants, that
they be left behind with their fathers in Pakistan, but if a mother
was not prepared for that she was allowed to take her child to
the Jalandar camp in India.

After reaching Jalandar such unmarried women always
found it embarrassing to face their relatives and acquaintances
with their infants. Whenever their relatives came to visit, they
would request the camp workers not to reveal that they had
children with them. These poor women were always faced
with this dilemma—on the one hand they were ready to go
back with their relatives, and on the other they were unable to
abandon their children. As long as they remained in the camp
they kept their infants with them all the time—they knew that
they would have to leave them behind once they left. They
would invariably request the social workers at the camp to
look after their children. "Be merciful to my child. Give him
milk on time and see that he does not cry. Will I ever be able
see my child agin? Who will bring him up? Who will look after
his education? What will his future be?" These were questions
we could not answer because we did not know what destiny
had in store for these children. To console them, however, we
gave suitable replies. At the moment of parting everyone wept
bitterly, knowing that it would not be possible to cry openly
once they rejoined their families. They had no alternative but
to forget that they had ever been mothers.

Most of the infants were healthy and good-looking. Perhaps they had inherited their good looks and fair complexions
from their parents who were brought up in the healthy climate
of Punjab. Separate arrangements were made for these children in Amritsar. There was one supervisor and one ayah for
two or three infants. Provisions were made for milk, baby food,
clothes and cradles.

They were kept in Amritsar for about two months. It took a long time befor a permanent home was established for them. Mridulaben always took a personal interest in their welfare. Whenever she visited Amritsar she invariably made it a point to inspect the Children's Home, and if she saw any lack in the arrangements she saw to it that it was removed without delay. However, despite all this care and attention most of the children started to lose weight after some time. When efforts to improve their health by providing additional vitamins and nutrition also failed, we realised the vital role a mother plays in the welfare of a child.

After some time Mridulaben succeeded in getting a separate ward for these children at the Kamla Nehru Hospital in Allahabad. The Government of India also agreed to assume full responsibility for them. Infants ranging from two to 12 months of age had been left behind in the Amritsar camp. The task of sending them to Allahabad proved to be a complicated affair. It took a long time for the management of the Indian Airlines to agree to take these infants free of charge. The procedure adopted was as follows: one of the social workers from our camp would place a couple of babies in a basket along with their clothes, milk, food, etc., and hand over the basket to the air hostess of a Delhi-bound plane. This would then be collected by social workers in Delhi who, in turn, took them from Delhi airport to Lady Hardinge Hospital. Next day the same basket was brought to the airport and sent on a flight to Allahabad. In Allahabad, social workers assigned to this special duty received them and then admitted them to their special ward. We used to send sealed envelopes with those children, with three copies of statements containing information regarding their date of birth, name of mother and father, and any other important information. We had given names to the infants.

We had made a number of promises to their mothers at the time of parting about how we would personally look after them, but these proved to be false as we ourselves could not see them again. Even today when I remember their mothers sobbing, my heart aches with sorrow.

Trauma & Triumph

HASNA SAHA

Hasna Saha was born in 1939 in Arkandi village, Faridpur district, in East Bengal. Like many others she crossed over to West Bengal after Partition in 1948, when she was only nine years old. A long and arduous struggle followed thereafter. She recalls her life after migrating to West Bengal—a life which records her trauma as well as her triumph.

No dictionary has ever indicated that the word 'Freedom' can be so cruel and heartless. We were village residents in East Bengal, but our village did not correspond to the stereotypical image that the term 'village' evokes. Even in 1930 it was thriving, with a railway station, a government-run dispensary, post office, school and seven-days-a-week market. Village life was full of joy and merry-making and the atmosphere was filled with a festive spirit all year round. The slowly meandering Chandana river still casts a magical spell on me. All the development work in our village was carried out under the supervision of my late father, Basanta Kumar Choudhary. Seen in the context of that time, he was an enlightened man with a modern and progressive outlook.

The uncertainty and utter confusion surrounding Independence and Partition that the newspapers regularly reported, depressed and saddened me. The elders frequently said, "It will no longer be possible to stay in this country." A sense of fear, of apprehension, haunted the mind. Partition came. My father's professional life continued uninterrupted, but a stray remark by the maulvi of the school broke the tranquility. Soon after Partition he informed the headmaster-moshaai or Principal, i.e., my father—"Master-moshaai, you will now have to learn the Islamic language, Urdu."

Our ancestral home was located in village Arkandi in the Goalando subdivision of Faridpur district in East Bengal. We neither heard about nor saw any acts of arson, looting, violence or rape being committed in our district, even during that tumultuous time, but that one sentence uttered by the maulvi upset my father so much that the very next day, leaving us all behind, he left the country. By himself. He took only a small tin suitcase and a battered cane-handle umbrella with him. This was some time at the end of 1947. Fortunately, the then subdivisional officer of Ranaghat in West Bengal found a job for my father in Cooper's Transit Camp. My mama (maternal uncle), on his way back home to Faridpur during the holidays, found my father sick and ill at the camp.

This news naturally upset my mother. After consulting my mama and getting his permission from my jethamoshai (father's elder brother), she started off for the camp with us—her six young children and didima (maternal grandmother) in tow. Naturally, it was an emotionally-charged dawn. As I walked down the ridge separating the paddy fields towards the railway station, I suddenly realised that this was my final exit from my beloved homeland; that the time had come to bid adieu forever. Tears streamed down my face, soaking my dress. The smiling faces of my childhood friends, Renu and Bina, flashed before my eyes. The thought of leaving Riziya, a Muslim girl, filled my heart with pain. Leaving everything behind, severing all connections, we reached our final destination—Chandmari Camp on the other side.

An altogether different life started in the camp. We did not get permanent accommodation on our arrival so, for the time being, we had to live in a tent. It was quite well-protected and guarded, but alas! we were now labelled as 'foreigners'. Whomever we tried to mix with seemed to come from a different world, mainly because their way of speaking, manners, customs—nothing matched ours. They spoke Bangla, but the tone and dialect were different. Still, one could easily feel an intense desire in both parties to interact and get to know each other. Within a few days of our arrival we found a pond nearby; Chandana river was lost to us forever, but we needed this pond to swim in and also play our very own version of water-polo. Okay, there may be no orchard here, but we didn't allow ourselves to get disheartened so easily. Soon we discovered the *kool* tree, as well as other climbers and creepers in the vicinity.

In the midst of this search for a carefree life, I was admitted to the local school. Our school offered ample opportunities for extra-curricular activities: games, music, dance, and so on. One memorable incident from my school days was the severe chiding we got from our mathematics teacher when we failed to solve a simple mathematical problem. His dialect was altogether unfamiliar to me—maybe that's why I actually enjoyed his scolding, because I was hearing this dialect for the first time! On the whole, along with the pain and loss, there was also a sense of satisfaction in discovering something new. My twin sister and I were awarded the first prize in drama at the annual function of the school, and this opened up new vistas for us.

The riot of Muladi in Barisal in 1950 made for an altogether new experience. The heart-rending cries of helpless children, young girls and half-naked women filled my heart with great pain and intense sorrow. Those who somehow survived the bestial torture arrived on this side—helpless, distressed, abused, harassed and humiliated. An eye-witness to this killing spree, young Shailo Sarkar, our next-door neighbour in the camp, often screamed during her sleep, "Help! Help! They have killed my father!" The rioters had hacked both her father and younger brother to death.

My father was transferred to Kashipur Camp and we finally arrived in Kolkata. After passing my high school examination from Surendranath Balika Vidyalaya in 1955, I was admitted to Surendranath Morning College. At this point, my elder sister found a job with the women's branch of the relief and reha- bilitation department of the state government. Her first post- ing was at Chamtaa Women's Camp in Krishnanagar. Through her we twin sisters found jobs in that camp as teacher and general assistant. This was on March 1, 1956.

Life now was altogether different. I was the general assist- ant in charge of nearly 210 families. Camp inmates were enti- tled to nine rupees, two annas in cash, two seers of rice, three seers of wheat and fourteen chhataks of dal every fortnight. Every day, they received a quarter seer of diluted cow's milk per head, and twice a year, clothes, blankets, etc. Free medical treatment to the sick and ailing was provided in the camp it- self. If necessary, the seriously ill were sent to government hospitals in Kolkata, and the entire cost of medicines and treat- ment was borne by the government. One-time help of Rs 700 was provided by the government to parents to marry off their daughters.

The official rule was that only families with women as heads would find shelter in the women's camps—no male member above the age of 18 was allowed to live in them. In fact, they were barred entry. I cannot give you the exact number of such camps, but I still recall a few—Ranaghat Women's Camp, Haringhata Women's Camp, Titagarh Women's Camp 2, Habra, Bansberia, Bhadrakali, Rupasree Palli, Pearadoba, Kashipur, Ananda Ashram Children's Home and Ashok Avenue Children's Home. These homes came under the supervision of the wom- en's wing of the relief and rehabilitation department. Camp inmates included women from affluent and well-off families from erstwhile East Bengal, with whom fate had played a cruel trick. For example, Snehalata Ghosh—daughter-in-law of the renowned mathematician, Deboprosad Ghosh—along with two sons and two daughters sought refuge in Chamtaa Camp. Her eldest daughter died while they were in the camp; the younger one was sent to Ananda Ashram, while her sons were admitted to the local school. The younger son joined the army and from there got admitted to a medical course. He is now an accomplished medical practitioner. Snehalata Ghosh was a gentle-natured, well-mannered lady, above all the meanness and intrigues that one usually associates with life in a camp. Even in the midst of abject poverty, she led a respectable and dignified life. But at the same time the irresponsible acts of girls like Bibha Biswas and Anima Das brought disrepute to the camp. They used to disappear for days, abandoning their children, only to return a day before government doles were distributed. Bibha ultimately got a job as an ayah in the Dhubulia Camp Hospital, while Anima joined as nurse after completing a course on nursing and midwifery.

There were many such uprooted women and men who never dreamt that a catastrophe called Partition would change their lives so drastically. Like Narayan Das. He arrived in his new home with his grandmother (not his own, but an elderly lady who used to live next door). He was one of the three boys that I got admitted to Narendrapur Ramakrishna Mission. He stood second in the higher secondary examination and is now a top-ranking bank officer. In fact, all three of them are now well-established.

I still remember that fateful night vividly. After tucking in her infant sons, Hena Chaudhuri went out for a chat nearby. Suddenly the tent, with the boys fast asleep inside, caught fire when a lantern placed near the cot fell down. People rushed to put the flames out; but, sadly, it was too late—one son had already died. The rest were admitted to government hospital in Krishnanagar. The second son died there. Hena was mad with grief. The two who survived this ghastly tragedy were sent to a children's home in Ashok Avenue. We spared no effort to help these hapless destitutes. I specially remember the efforts of the superintendent of our Home, Shantikana Sen, and her compassion and skill.

In 1960, I got an opportunity to participate in a jamboree organised by the Bharat Scouts and Guides in Bangalore. It was an international event. The five-day camp was a great experience for me, and later I joined the organisation as a permanent employee. Here, I came to know that Bakul Chakraborty, one of the inmates of the Titagarh Home, had gone to London to participate in an international camp convened by the Guides, while another refugee, Tulu Das, became the first recipient of the President's Guide Award in West Bengal.

In October, 1964, I joined the Koraput Sonabeda Camp set up in Dandakaranya to conduct a training course for guide captains. Along with the local girls, many refugee girls, too participated in the training programmes. Our temporary accommodation was just next to the refugee camp. I was assisted by Usha Ganguly (a relative of the former Mayor of Kolkata, Mihir Ganguly), Mira Ganguly, a teacher from Kolkata, P.S. Parida and Nihar Nalini Swain from Orissa.

One day Mr Das, the superintendent, requested me to make a plea to the refugees against desertion. I started my speech— "Respected inmates, I, too, am an uprooted refugee, perhaps the daughter of one of your relatives. The only difference between you and me is that, while you are lucky enough to be given a place of permanent residence and other facilities for leading a decent life, I have to roam from place to place to manage two square meals a day for myself and my family." At the end of the meeting, many inmates came up to me and promised that they would not desert the camp. I must emphasise that the environment and climate of Koraput were ideal for building a prosperous community.

My work as a girl guide has brought me in close contact with many Muslim families. I have always treated them as my own. One with whom I share a very close relationship is Ashrafi Begum. Even today, whenever she comes to India from

Bangladesh, she never forgets to call me. The general secretary of Bangladesh Girl Guides Association, Jinnat Apa, is like my own elder sister. Noorinessa Begum—Noor di to me—treats my husband like her own elder brother. How can I be a Muslim-hater after all the love and respect that have been bestowed on me?

Bangladesh is my motherland. I can never consider it a foreign country because our language is the same, but I have no intention of visiting it, because the fond memories that I treasure of my motherland are the only possession I am left with. I do not want to lose them.

I applaud the architects of Partition for carving out two warring factions—East Pakistan and West Pakistan. It was we, the lesser mortals, who became the pawns in this dirty power-game and whose lives were shattered. Many are still adrift on either side of the border, in search of a shelter. The time is ripe for some introspection—to look back and take an objective view of what happened in the past so that history does not repeat itself.

As told to Subhoranjan Dasgupta, and translated from Bengali by Subhasree Ghosh and Subhoranjan Dasgupta.

Subhoranjan Dasgupta, a well-known writer on political and social issues, is a Senior Fellow, School of Women's Studies, Jadavpur University, Kolkata.

Lady Camp Commandant

JOGENDRA SINGH

Jogendra Singh was in her final year of M.A. at Government College, Lahore, when Partition took place. She first went to Ambala in August 1947, then to Dehradun. She served in refugee camps at Karnal and Kurukshetra, where she was Camp Commandant for some years. This interview took place in Karnal in 1989.

In March 1947 riots took place in Lahore. The riots had first started in Rawalpindi, but they had their repercussions in Lahore. We were sent back home from the University in March '47. The exams were to take place in April but they were postponed. We still studied at home. I lived in Sargodha till August and then I was evacuated. Many of my cousins had already left. We went to Dehradun because one of my cousins who had studied in Kinnaird college lived there—her husband was posted in Dehradun. So my brother and I were sent. My uncle was already there. Different family members came through different routes and means, and then we contacted each other through radio, letters, somehow conveyed messages. One day I got a letter from my father in Amritsar saying he had reached there with a truck convoy.

I had come by air with my youngest brother. Some Indian Airlines or Bharat Airlines or something. We landed in Amritsar in late August 1947. Partition had just taken place. We were not sure what would happen. Father, Mother and four younger sisters came to Dehradun in December. I had started studying for my exams but I saw an ad in the papers for a Lady Camp Commandant's job. I got the job at Jalandar.

Wasn't it unusual to see an ad and go?

No, it was not unusual—we were all looking for things to do. We listened to the radio for such things. Instead of giving my exams I decided to take up the job. The salary was Rs. 450, which was not a small sum in 1947. Government wanted people to work in these camps so they paid well. It was a full-fledged government job. This was Punjab government. I was posted at Karnal Camp. Premwati Thapar was the person in-charge of this work. Miss Makhan Singh and I were interviewed together, both of us were posted at Karnal. The largest camps were in this area, Kurukshetra was a large camp. My husband (we were not married then) was officer-in-charge of all the camps in Karnal Distt. He put me in charge of this camp and Miss Makhan Singh of the other camp in Karnal.

How many people were there in the camps at their peak?

I do not have an exact idea, I have also forgotten the numbers. It must have been more than ten lakhs in all. Every time trainloads of people came. Our work was to enroll the arrivals, provide board and lodging, see to it that they got cots to sleep on, wood to cook, etc. Army was there, but these were run by the Central and Punjab governments. My husband knows facts and figures. Gradually people made arrangements to go to their relations, got jobs, and started leaving the camps. The strength of the camps slowly declined, then the two camps were consolidated into one camp. After one and a half years I was shifted to Hansi, there was a camp there also. Then I went to another camp in Panipat where I was fully in charge.

In between I prepared for my exams, and in April 1948 I went to Ludhiana government college.

Where did you stay while you worked in the camp?

There was a house near the camp, behing the DC's house. I took a room in that annexe. In Panipat I stayed in the camp in a room with an improvised bathroom. My parents came to stay with me in that room for a couple of months, and then I shifted them to Dehradun. I had a maid from the camp to cook for me. She was a widow with a child. Later on I rehabilitated her.

After that, Sucheta Kripalani, who used to come often, dragged me to 7 Jantar Mantar Road, Delhi. I worked with her there and she started a knitting and sewing centre. Then in Curzon Road I organised work for women where they would do tailoring, embroidery etc. In Purana Qila also there was a centre. Uma Kapoor also worked with her and later she joined the Cottage Industries Emporium.

Then Mrs. Kripalani shifted me to Lucknow, where we rented a big building and taught refugee women tailoring and embroidery and gave them work for a living. We would give them weekly wages. Sadiq Ali, who became Congress President, also lived there. Well-off Lucknow women helped us sell the products, got us orders for our work.

After Lucknow I got married, in 1949 January, and came to Karnal. I did not work for a few years, then I joined Mrs. Anand and started a social welfare society.

Did you know about Mrs. Anand's home where she had 50 widows right in the beginning?

Yes, yes, I stayed with her for some time. We had a common kitchen. There was the United Council for Relief and Welfare, and a half-built house where she worked. Later on most of the widows from her home went to the Ashram. Once women got jobs and their children got educated, the government stopped giving them stipends.

What kind of women were they?

They were mostly lower middle class women, some from towns, some from villages. Some were from farming families, some from goldsmiths... Some said they had lots of land and property in Pakistan. Some of them got compensations—one of my maids got a house in Panipat as compensation. I helped her get this and withdrew her from the camp. Later she sold that property and put the money in the bank. I helped her with that, too.

There were very few women from well-off families. The rare well-off woman who lost all her relations might have come to the camp, but she would leave soon after she got compensation or found some relative...

Women from good families didn't go out to work, they worked in the Ashram only. Some of them asked for a lump-sum to get settled, and left the Ashram.

Training was provided to women in cane work, chair-making, chic-making, machine embroidery, etc. We ran schools for children, adult education classes were run for women. Two daughters of a well-off local family came to the Ashram to help.

When I left the Ashram in 1948 there were more than 3000-4000 people there, about 2000 families.

Were there any women who had been abducted and recovered?

Yes, there were, but they couldn't come out in the open. We had to draw them out. I don't remember the names now. There was a Muslim Transit Camp here at the end of 1947, people going to Pakistan would be brought to it. We used to provide rations to them also. In that Muslim camp women used to complain to us that they had been molested by the drivers, etc.

Our women from Sheikhupura, which was a criminal district., told us that their jewellery was taken away, their clothes removed... A number of abortions were done in the camp also, which we kept a closely guarded secret so that no one would find out about them and they wouldn't have difficulties in the future. Abortion was illegal at that time, but we had a doctor. The circumstances were such that we had to do this, otherwise the women might have committed suicide. All this was done behind closed doors.

Were there many such cases?

Some women had it done themselves. We got about 30 per cent women like this. Some were married, some unmarried. There were women who had one child in the lap and were pregnant again. When we asked them they told us it happened on the way. Mostly they were from Sheikhupura and other areas. Some of them were treated badly, but others said they had been saved by Muslims, were given refuge in Muslim homes. Muslims treated them like sisters and mothers. There were others who took them home and then raped them. What you see in the T.V. serial *Tamas*, actually happened.

There were no family planning methods at that time, no one talked about it openly, no one went to doctors, so we used to call midwives here to get the work done. Sometimes when women didn't have money to pay the midwives we paid from our own pockets. After my marriage I had three women sterilized in my garage, they were two months pregnant. One woman who worked as a maid in a home in Karnal was made pregnant. She had been raped by the servant in that household. I took her to my garage, told the Ashram that she had cholera and should not stay in the camp. I kept her in my garage and called a midwife. We did it all on paper—my husband helped me with this.

Were the women molested while they were in the Ashram?

Of course it happened to many, they used to return late from work. But most cases were of wilful consent. They used to tell us it was done against their will, but this was not always true. We investigated. But it was natural, they also had instincts. A woman did it to have a good time and sometimes conceived. There was nothing wrong with it. After all they were also human, and human instincts are the same the world over. They were young, their husbands had died, they had nothing in life. How could they survive? I took a very broad view of these things, although at that time we had to keep all this a secret.

Even now old Ashramites come to me. One of them still works in the hospital, roams around like a powerful chowdhrain. She used to tell me lots of stories. I have forgotten her name, but she was from Sheikhupura. After she left the camp, she built a house for herself, she is quite well-off now.

Many women used to abort themselves using local methods, giving things to drink, giving medicines. There were many midwives amongst them. Sometimes, in pain, women would shout loudly, cursing those men who had done it to them. When we asked them why they were cursing, they replied, "Bibiji, what do you know what we have gone through, what we have suffered."

But many women got remarried. Some we got remarried in the camp. Even today in Karnal there is a short-stay home, women come there. We got two of them married last week to two peons, with proper dowries. This is through the Social Welfare Board.

When you were in the Ashram, was there any system of keeping records, files of the women?

There used to be a record about their families, how they came to the camp. We had to find all this out before giving them admission. Trainloads used to come, normally a group was from the same village or mohalla, they knew each other. We were there to do all this work, to fill the proformas. Rehabilitation Department of the Government of Jalandar used to have these records but they must have been destroyed by now. One copy remained with us in the camp, one went to the government of India, one to Jalandar. Now I don't know where they would be. Punjab and Haryana also got divided, so I don't know.

What was the routine in the camp?

We used to go at nine in the morning, take a round of the camp to see if the chulha-chowkas were clean, children had gone to school, the ailing people had been attended to. If someone died, we saw to it that that person got a proper funeral according to his or her religious rites, was the night peaceful, no theft, no eve-teasing... all this also happened, we had our own police/chowkidar.

We used to give them quilts, some of them sold them in the market. We had to control all this. We used to go on looking till 7 pm. We had to go for rounds at night also, to check everything.

On Sundays we used to go for prayer meetings. Some did hawans, others prayed in the gurudwara. Everyone joined each other on festivals. Since there were 4000-5000 people, there were several gurudwaras.

There were male inmates also in the camp, families lived there. In the Ashrams there were no men, only young boys were allowed. Once the boys grew up, they had to leave the Ashram.

There were no common kitchens?

No, but when the trains came we organised langars. We asked every family to make eight extra rotis for the langar. There was no government staff for cooking. We made small packets and fed them, gave rations to each family, dals, atta, vegetables, oil, etc. Common kitchens were not possible, it was very difficult to organise that... Newcomers were able to cook for themselves after two or three days, when they were given all supplies.

Sometimes we used to get orders from the financial commissioner not to take any new inmates, but when new groups came we were not able to say no.

I was very strict and I managed the camps with a lot of discipline. People had small conflicts about small things, petty thefts, children fighting, etc., we had to manage all this. In winter we put rice husk on the floor and put out mattresses.

We found several skilled people in the camps, cobblers, halwais, cooks. They started their own work which also helped the camps. They started making pakoras, someone started a barber shop to make a living, tailors started stitching clothes for others. Women also started enterprises and we helped them. We did a survey to ask what skills women had, then we gave them raw materials to make papad, or achaar, paid them for their labour and used these things for the camp.

One day, what I did was, I was in-charge of this camp, my husband was overall-in-charge, we decided to get married. I got a complaint about some men who had done some theft, one of them had even pulled my plait from outside the window. I had them arrested. My husband was so amused listening to this. He was also the magistrate. He asked me what authority I had to have people arrested. They will have to be brought to his court, he said, and I would also have to appear. I said I am not coming to your court. Anyway, at night he took me there and made them apologise to me. So such cases went on all the time.

— *Interviewed by Kamla Bhasin and Ritu Menon*

Rehabilitation, East & West

PHULRENU GUHA

Phulrenu Guha was born in 1931. Political activist and tireless social worker, she was Minister of State, Social Welfare, in Indira Gandhi's Cabinet. She helped the refugees of 1947, specially women, in their heroic struggle for self-sufficiency. Dr Guha is one of those few politicians who has earned respect from all quarters for her selfless devotion to the cause of women's empowerment.

Y ou have first-hand knowledge about the struggle of East Bengali refugees who settled in the Andamans. What was the outcome of their struggle?

On our first visit to the Andamans in the (nineteen) Sixties, we were provided a launch by the government, and so we had the unique opportunity of touring different clusters of islands. We saw the various settlements set up by the refugees from East Bengal, saw how they had adapted marvellously to the new set-up. The natural beauty of the Andamans is no less than that of Bangladesh, in fact many regions are even more beautiful than East Bengal. The children of the settlers studied in schools opened specially to cater to their needs. On the whole, East Bengalis led a happy and productive life. They informed us in one voice that their decision to migrate to the Andamans, rather than stay back in the refugee colonies in

West Bengal, had enabled them to look forward to a better future.

What I want to say is, the Communist Party of India never realised the irreparable damage they caused by objecting to the transfer of refugees to these islands—the Andamans could really have emerged as a second East Bengal. When the refugees started to migrate, the island was sparsely populated. Had they migrated en masse many would not have had to endure the hardships of the refugee colonies. At the same time, the newly developed society and community in Andamans could have taken the shape of a resurgent East Bengal. As someone who originally hails from East Bengal, I still nurse this grievance against the Communists.

You were the Secretary of United Council of Relief and Welfare—how did this organisation help displaced refugees?

Even now, I frankly cannot figure out why I was chosen to be Secretary of this organisation. Anyway, it was a huge affair—shiploads of milk arrived, as well as clothing, we had to unload and store all this relief material. Old, second-hand dress material that was sent by foreign donor nations was often useable but, unfortunately, some were unsuitable because they were far too large. We had to quickly arrive at an agreement with some of the women's organisations (which were set up during that time to help refugees) that they would alter these dresses so that they could be worn by the impoverished children of refugees.

There is a small history behind the spread and growth of these organisations. The government would purchase clothes from various sources and give them to the refugees. We calculated that if we ourselves produced the dresses, the prices would be lower than what the government was then spending on buying them. The government also regularly handed out doles. We decided that instead of accepting dole, a new workplan should be implemented. It was like this—we would hand over the dresses that we tailored to the government and the government would give us what it spent on them. In other words, refugee women would both tailor and stitch the clothes—blouses, petticoats, shirts, trousers, etc.—and we would pay them for the work done. This helped many of these destitute girls to become self-sufficient. And so at least two women's organisations came into being in Jadavpur. With their self-generated resources and funds, the women constructed their own buildings—they even managed to set up a maternity home from their own resources and our contributions. This new system which opted for remuneration instead of dole enabled the poor refugees to rightfully acquire just recognition for their work, while subsidies helped them to earn in a dignified and decent way. You know, the system of doles saps the vital urge to work and erodes self-respect. I can claim this from what I saw and experienced.

Have you ever penned your experiences and thoughts with regard to the rehabilitation of refugees?

Not all, but bits and pieces may be found in my book, *Elo Melo Money Elo* (Random Thoughts that came to My Mind), but I will have to revise it. Fortunately, the person who has undertaken the task of revising the material is familiar with my work. My organisation helped him and his refugee colony a lot. He chided me once saying, "You haven't written anything about your work!" There are bits and pieces in my book, but I know that a more detailed description is necessary.

From your book, we know about the two maternity homes that you were instrumental in setting up—one in Nakashipara and the other in Harthuba—for parturient women. Could you describe the Harthuba home: is it still in operation?

The name of the place is Harthuba. Sadly, the Nakashipara home doesn't exist anymore but the one in Harthuba is still functioning, not only as a maternity home, its activities have branched out in other directions as well. In fact, it has emerged

as a full-fledged institution. Even today, you may meet a few
refugee women there, but with the passage of time most of
them have become very old and perhaps a bit senile. You will
be lucky if you find children whose childhoods were spent as
refugees in West Bengal. After crossing the Habra railway station, proceed towards Bonogram, take the left-hand road and
you will see a sign pointing towards Harthuba.

> *We know that compared to Punjab, the number of rape
> cases in East Bengal were not that many. But in that home
> for parturient women that you just spoke about, do you
> recall the presence of any woman who had become preg-
> nant after being raped?*

Those who had become pregnant as a result of being raped
did not come to this home. My personal opinion is that not
many rapes took place in East Bengal—a few instances do occur
even now, and it happened during those days also! The general practice is to destroy the child born of rape... but I do
remember one particular instance when a girl, in spite of family pressure, refused to abort the child. She gave birth and
brought up her child. After her mother died I lost track of this
girl, but I still remember her determination and resilience.

> *During those turbulent days in 1946 you visited Noakhali,
> met Mahatma Gandhi—do you feel that it was after
> Noakhali that Gandhi realised that Partition was inevi-
> table?*

Noakhali was followed by the gruesome carnage in Bihar.
Gandhi might have had some idea of the inevitable after
Noakhali, but he also realised that the so-called solution of
Partition would not ensure peace and tranquility. As for me, I
was dead against Partition. But after seeing what Suhrawardy
did in Kolkata on August 16, 1946 (Direct Action Day) I felt
that perhaps Partition would bring some good, at least some
peace. But Gandhiji was a stalwart, he correctly assessed that
Partition would not guarantee peace. We, the common people, failed to understand this. You see, although the prevalent

belief is that the main arbiter of Partition was Md. Ali Jinnah, I personally feel it was Suhrawardy who was responsible for the division in the east.

What specific incidents from Noakhali do you still remember? What did you see there?

Those who were forcibly kept in different refugee camps in Noakhali were given *chiraa* or flattened rice to eat—that was the very first time in my life that I heard that if you soak *chiraa* in water it turns into something like cooked rice. Two women who were about to have this meal of flattened rice turned red in the face because they suspected that their meal had been touched by somebody from a lower caste. They said they would become outcastes if they consumed this 'contaminated food'. Some of their fellow inmates chided them and said, "You rubbed shoulders with Muslims, you came here, you didn't lose your caste then; why fear it now?"—I still recall this particular incident. Here I must add that women in Noakhali faced a lot of suffering—molestation, rape, forced conversion and marriages, though the scale and intensity of such atrocities was much greater in Punjab.

This recollection provokes a crucial question—why did Partition happen at all? You have mentioned two things in your book: first, had Fazlul Haq joined the Congress, Partition could have been avoided; second, due to the tyranny of high caste Hindus, the low caste Hindus of Barisal converted to Christianity en masse. On the whole, which factor would you select as the most important for Partition—the nitty-gritty of everyday life, scarred by untouchability, which the Muslims resented, or developments on the larger political front following the exploitation of Muslims by Hindu zamindars?

To me, the root-cause of Partition was the erosion of fraternal feeling among the people of undivided Bengal. I still remember an elderly Muslim gentleman—if I were adept in painting, I could have sketched him and shown you—sitting on his balcony, calmly telling me, "If a pariah dog enters a Hindu household, they throw away the drinking water stored in the earthen pitcher; but when we enter, not only the water, the whole earthen pitcher is thrown away." I didn't know this. No such custom was practised in our home, but after thorough cross-checking, I was convinced that he was speaking the truth. This exploitation, this disrespect, this was the most potent cause.

> *You had a debate with Mridula Sarabhai regarding the repatriation of abducted women. Mahavir Tyagi maintained that those who had settled down and started life anew, uprooting them once again would be unwise... Do you recall that debate?*

I enjoyed a very warm and cordial relationship with Mridula Sarabhai. When the issue of the repatriation of Hindu women living in West Pakistan came to the fore, she asked me to come down to New Delhi with a view to bringing these girls back. This sparked off a heated debate between us. I told her that the girls were leading a protected life there with their new families and children. After forcing them to forsake everything once again and bringing them here, would she be able to compensate their second loss? God knows, they may be forced to spend the rest of their lives in refugee camps. Nobody will volunteer to marry them, even their own families will not take them back. I said that if anybody voluntarily wishes to cross over to this side, it is acceptable, but nobody should be forced to do so. Mridula advocated forced repatriation throughout. The debate hinged on this issue mainly. Man is not an inanimate object to be carried from one place and deposited in another, again and again. One should always look at the psychological aspect. She might be able to leave her husband, but what about her child? Any child is a part and parcel of herself, her very being, and reason for existence. Every mother enjoys a very special bond with her children because they are born of her flesh and blood...

Partition, relief, rehabilitation—you were actively in-volved in all these. Do you believe that the refugees of West Punjab enjoyed preferential treatment?

There are two points that I wish to make about this blatant partiality. The large scale and wanton massacre of innocents in the West left a deep scar on the public mind. The East, fortunately, did not have to experience such gross acts of inhuman violence. In the West you saw the carnage with your own eyes, in the East you heard what had already happened behind your back. Now these two experiences had a different effect on the human consciousness and mind. In the East, it was more a case of slow poisoning and so its effect was not that immediate, whereas in the West they were forced to see everything with their own eyes—murder, rape, loot, arson. This is a very important factor that somewhat accounts for the discrimination. The other reason is that since all the leaders of the East were located really far from the centre of political power, they could not breathe down the central government's neck and force them to render assistance. There is still another reason. Many, after leaving their families in erstwhile East Bengal, sought refuge in West Bengal but were in constant touch with their relatives in East Pakistan. New Delhi was well informed about these connections—the espionage system, being a direct legacy of the days of the Imperial Raj, was at its peak in those days. But even after giving all these reasons I will say that blatant discrimination did take place.

Discrimination prevailed in spite of Dr Bidhan Chandra Roy's most sincere efforts. In that context, we notice the epic struggle of the godforsaken Bengali refugees, especially the womenfolk. Armed with ordinary kitchen utensils, they valiantly resisted the hired goons of the rich landlords. But it is very unfortunate that this epic struggle which took place not far from Kolkata proper—in Jadavpur—has not found a favourable response from modern writers. What is your opinion on this?

Obviously, the writers themselves will be able to answer this better than I can—I am only an ordinary grassroot-level worker. But I will continue to speak of this struggle. As long as I am fortunate enough to live, I will perform this duty unwaveringly. Even after having lost everything, refugee women refused to end up on the losing side for a second time. Their struggle changed their lives. For the very first time they came out of the secluded precincts of their households. How could they have taken this gigantic step? Actually, the sheer struggle for survival and the taste of freedom propelled them forward.

> *After such an active and eventful life, when you look back on those days, do you remember any particular refugee woman whose suffering and struggles affect you even today?*

Yes, Sarajubala Sen. I still remember her. At the fag end of her eventful life she came to live in Jhargram, Midnapur. She was an illiterate village woman, Mashima (auntie) to everybody. Nobody can ever forget her immense suffering, her exemplary sacrifice, her valiant struggle for the uplift of downtrodden Bengali women. She was the spirit behind the setting up of a number of looms for women refugees. I remember her distinctly.

Interviewed by Subhoranjan Dasgupta, translated from Bengali by Subhasree Ghosh and Subhoranjan Dasgupta.